# HOME COOKING FOR MONEY

**Also by Judy Ridgway**

The Vegetarian Gourmet
Barbecues
Salad Days
The Vegetable Year Cookbook
Running your own Winebar

**With Ursula Garner**
Running your own Catering Company

**With Alan Curthoys**
Man in the Kitchen

# HOME COOKING FOR MONEY

## Judy Ridgway

PIATKUS

©1983 Judy Ridgway

First published in 1983
by Judy Piatkus (Publishers) Limited
5 Windmill Street, London W1
Reprinted in 1983
Reprinted 1986, updated

British Library Cataloguing in Publication Data

Ridgway, Judy
    Home cooking for money
    1. Food service management – Great Britain
    2. Small businesses – Great Britain – Management
    I. Title
    647′.95′068      TX911.3.M27

    ISBN 0–86188–221–0


Drawings by Eljay Crompton
Design by Paul Saunders

Typesetting by Phoenix Photosetting Ltd, Chatham
Printed and bound by Mackays of Chatham Ltd

# Contents

# Introduction

My first venture into professional cooking was very much a 'spur of the moment' event. An office friend and I had been pipe-dreaming about running our own catering company when a colleague came into the room and asked if we could recommend a good caterer for a small private dinner she was organising. 'Yes,' I said, 'we will do it.' My partner-to-be looked horror-struck but did not demur, and so there we were, plunged into menu planning, pricing, check lists and our very first dinner party!

From the beginning I thoroughly enjoyed professional cooking. After all, what more can you ask than to be paid for doing something that you enjoy.

Home cooking for money can be organised to suit you and your life style. However much time or capital you have available – or however little – there is sure to be something that you might like to do. The choice ranges from small-scale baking for market stalls and specialist activities such as cake decorating to running large-scale home preserving or outside catering operations.

This book looks at all the areas of cooking that can be developed as money-making concerns. The first four chapters deal with the practical, financial and legal aspects of cooking for money and with the marketing and selling of your product or service.

Since that first dinner party I have tried my hand at many of the activities covered in the book. I have also talked to all sorts of people who have been successful in their chosen area.

I would particularly like to thank Mrs N. Bloore, WI market organiser for Tiverton; Mrs V. Davies, WI market organiser for Ruislip; Jan Collier-Marsh; Jean Pierre Depesme, Jean Pierre's Pantry; Ursula Garner, Gluttons; Mrs Mary Grace; Hilary Kirsch; Janet Raglan; James Waghorn, Dartington Farm Foods; Angela Wilson Ward and Julian Worster for the time which they have made available to me and for their patience in answering my many questions.

A very special thank you, too, to my ex-partner Jane Atkinson for the happy and busy times we spent together in London Cooks, without which I would never have been able to write this book.

*Judy Ridgway*

# 1

# Considering what to do

Earning money by cooking from home can be flexible enough to suit almost everyone. If you can only work part-time, you could take up cake decorating, bake for a market stall or make confectionery and petit fours. On the other hand, if you have ambitions to build a full-time business, you could set up a freezer service, run a party catering operation, specialise in preparing office lunches and picnic boxes or in making and selling country foods.

Whatever you decide to do, you must realise from the start that working from home is not like going out to work. The discipline of set hours is missing and you will have to motivate yourself to work. This may be quite easy for the first few weeks, but once the initial enthusiasm has worn off you will still need to put in a certain number of hours and this may mean forcing yourself to work when you are feeling tired or miserable, or perhaps when the children are ill in bed. Delaying tactics will tend to creep in, however much you like cooking or are keen on your business. Some days you may feel that the family washing or mending a broken toy is much more important than cooking another batch of chutney, sorting out the month's accounts or getting down to composing some much needed promotional material. Banish these feelings as soon as they occur.

Try to arrange your life so that there is plenty of room for family, friends and work activities.

The rewards to be gained from working at home are certainly worth the effort. You can choose you own hours and work at your own pace – and there is no ill-tempered boss breathing down your neck. Last, but by no means least, making a profit by your own hard work brings very real satisfaction.

## WHAT CAN YOU DO?

You do not have to be a trained cook to sell the products of your kitchen. Of course, if you have had some sort of training it may be that bit easier to get started. What you do need to have is plenty of imagination, lots of energy and the ability to cope with the unexpected. You will also need to have a skill or a special idea to offer or to be a good all-round cook.

Sit down and ask yourself the following questions. Try to be as objective as possible. Use your notes to produce a list of things which you might be able to do or might like to do in order of feasibility.

*Do you have any special training?*
Answers might include a full-time catering course, a residential cookery course, a specialist course on Cordon Bleu cooking, cake decorating or chocolate work, a night school class in preserving, bread making or general cooking. But don't worry if the answer is 'no', just carry on and look at the next questions.

*Do you have any special skills?*
Some skills will be quite obvious; either you are good at cake decorating or raised pastry work or you are not. However, if you have not tried these activities you will need to think carefully about whether you are good at the sort of precise, rather fiddly work that they involve.

If you are not really sure how to answer this question, think about the aspects of your cookery which your family and friends particularly enjoy. Do you have a reputation for making super cakes? Do people gobble up your chocolate truffles or ask you for the recipes for your jams and marmalades? Do you like making chutneys, pâtés, quiches or homemade sausages?

The answers, whatever they are, will give you an indication of the areas that you should be thinking about. It doesn't matter if you only come up with one or two items. You can always develop more ideas to match the ones at which you excel.

Other points to consider include the amount of entertaining you undertake at home and the form that this takes. Do you revel in producing elaborate dinners, or do you prefer informal entertaining? Does the idea of a party for fifty or a hundred act as a challenge to your cooking ability or throw you into a flat panic? Do you think that other people would like the sort of things that you do.

### *Do you have any special inclinations?*
What do you enjoy cooking? However good you may be at making certain things, if you do not enjoy doing them there is absolutely no point in planning to spend a good deal of your time making them for sale.

Think about whether you are happy batch cooking or whether you would prefer to be doing something different each day. Do you think you would be happy working in someone else's kitchen, or would you prefer to stay in your own?

### *How much time do you have available?*
The answer to this question is quite easy if you have been working full-time up to this point and want to continue doing so from home. But if you have young children or elderly or infirm relations living with you, then the free time you have available will be limited.

It is very important to make as realistic an assessment as possible of the time you will be able to put into your business. There is no point in starting off with big ambitions, spending money on special

11

equipment and then finding that you do not have sufficient time to do a good job.

If your time is very limited, there are still plenty of things that you can do. The list includes cooking for WI markets, which are run under the auspices of the National Federation of Women's Institutes. The advantage of these markets is that you do not have to find sales outlets yourself; selling is taken care of for you by the market. You could also make preserves, or country foods such as raised pies, pâtés and sausages for sale through local shops, or prepare food for wine bars or pubs in your neighbourhood. A very small-scale cake decorating or frozen foods service might just fit in with your already busy schedule.

For those who do have plenty of time to spare, it is still important to decide how much effort you are prepared to make. There is no point starting to make regular supplies of a particular item, only to find that the quantities involved will take up more time to produce than you are willing to give.

### How flexible can you be?

The question of flexibility is an important one. Obviously, if you cannot easily leave the house or if you do not want to work in the evenings, an outside catering business is probably not for you. Outside catering can mean leaving home at the crack of dawn to set up a buffet at the races, or working long past midnight clearing up after an evening party or reception.

However, it is possible to run a catering business which fits in with your life style. One company I know specialises in business lunches and the owner has sufficient clients to ensure that she does not have to work in the evenings.

Another home cook friend specialises in cooking for dinner parties. She has three young children and organises her work pattern to fit in with the family. She cooks in the morning when the children are at school, and then takes the youngest child shopping with her in the early afternoon. The late afternoon is kept free for the children, and she finishes preparing, delivers and, if necessary,

serves the dinner in the evening. On Saturday her husband helps with the children and Sunday is kept free for the family. It has proved an ideal arrangement.

The other business opportunities open to the home cook can largely be carried out without leaving home, provided that the business remains on a fairly small scale. Shopping and delivering are the only outside activities which have to be fitted in.

You should now be able to prepare a list of possible money making activities, in order of feasibility. But have you considered everything that you could do? The following check lists show foods to make and services to offer which are suitable for either very small-scale production or larger-scale production.

**Small-scale Activities**

| Foods and services | Relevant chapters | Foods and services | Relevant chapters |
|---|---|---|---|
| Biscuits | 5, 8 | Pastries | 5, 7 |
| Bread | 5 | Pâtés and terrines | 5, 7, 10 |
| Cakes and buns | 5 | Petit fours | 8 |
| Cake decorating | 9 | Pickles | 5, 6 |
| Chocolates | 8 | Quiches | 5, 10 |
| Chutney | 5, 6 | Raised pies | 5, 7, 10 |
| Crystallised fruits | 8 | Sausages and brawn | 5, 7 |
| Desserts | 10 | Savoury dishes | 10 |
| Dinner parties | 13 | Smoked foods | 7 |
| Fruits in alcohol | 5, 6 | Soft cheese and goats' cheese | 5, 7 |
| Fudge | 8 | Toffee | 8 |
| Jams and marmalades | 5, 6 | Truffles | 8 |
| Ketchups and sauces | 5, 6 | | |

**Large-scale Activities**

| Foods and services | Relevant chapters | Foods and services | Relevant chapters |
|---|---|---|---|
| Cake decorating | 9 | Lunches | 12–14 |
| Dinner parties | 13 | Parties | 14 |
| Frozen foods | 11 | Picnics | 12, 14 |
| General cooking | 10–14 | Weddings | 14 |

## Market Research

Is there a market in your area for the activities on your list? After all, there is no point in deciding to specialise in wedding breakfasts or in making wedding cakes if the area is full of retired people. And it would be equally futile trying to sell very expensive chocolates in an area where most people are on a tight budget!

To find out whether you will be able to sell the foods and services on your list you will need to do a little basic market research.

Start by deciding on your catchment area. Draw a circle on the map outlining the area within which you could easily travel to deliver goods or to cater for dinners and parties. Next, try to assess that area in terms of spending power and tastes. To help you do this, answer the following questions about the area as fully as possible.

*'No, I don't do much entertaining here.'*

### Is the area a wealthy one?
Are the inhabitants likely to be able to afford luxury foods or to employ outside caterers? A chat with one or two local estate agents or a local council official will help you to identify more expensive areas.

### What sort of people live there?

Are they young people with young families, middle-aged people with grown-up families or is it a retirement area? Remember that different groups will have different requirements and different tastes.

### What potential sales outlets are there?

Your list should include markets, specialist grocers and butchers, delicatessens, tea rooms and cafés, wine bars, pubs and gift or souvenir shops in your area. (See chapter 4.)

### What sort of businesses are there?

Try to assess what the outside catering requirements of local businesses might be. Do any of the businesses have a company shop?

### Is there any competition?

If so, can the area support more than one supplier in the same field?

You should now be able to finalise your list of possible money-making actitivies, but beware of shortening your list too much. If you start off with only one speciality and you have guessed wrong, the results will be very discouraging. Keep a fairly open mind and use your research as a guideline. It is sensible to begin by offering a range of complementary products or services, specialising only when you see a pattern of profitable work emerging.

When I started London Cooks, we were prepared to do almost anything at all! We took on small lunches and dinners as well as large buffets and wedding breakfasts, and we even threw in a freezer service as well. But as the business grew we cut out the smaller, less profitable functions and now, with one or two exceptions for customers of long standing, we will only cater for thirty plus.

Similarly, another small business I know decided to specialise in home preserves and started off by offering jams, marmalades, chutneys and pickles. The jams turned out to be by far the most popular line and so now the owner concentrates on a range of unusual jams and has stopped making the other items.

# COURSES AND QUALIFICATIONS

Once you have decided on the sort of produce or service you might offer for sale, it is time to study the relevant legislation (chapter 3) and to take another look at your own skills. How long is it since you last had any training? Are you out of practice in any area? Are you really sure that you can cope with all the items that might be required by a demanding hostess? This sort of assessment could point the way to some intensive practice or maybe to a refresher course or even to a more comprehensive training course.

So what courses can you take and how do you find out about them?

*Private Cookery Schools*
There are a number of private schools operating in different parts of the country. They vary both in the type of cooking that is taught and in the length of the courses. Sabine de Mirbeck's Ecole de Cuisine Française in Sussex, for example, offers anything from short intensive courses of one to three weeks' duration to a full year's course split into the usual three terms. Divertimenti in London offers short seminars on cooking. Both these, along with the Cordon Bleu School in London and the Marie Tante School of Cookery in Woking, specialise in French cooking. But there are other courses available, like Kenneth Lo's Chinese Cookery School and Claudia Roden's Middle Eastern Cookery.

For the names and addresses of cookery schools, look in your local Yellow Pages or send a stamped addressed envelope to The

Good Housekeeping Institute, National Magazine House, 72 Broadwick Street, London W1V 28P for the *Good Housekeeping* up-to-date list of schools.

## Holiday Courses

Several women's magazines run their own short cookery courses and these are sometimes set in interesting places in France or in other European countries. These holiday courses are fun to go on; they can help to widen your repertoire of dishes and generally stimulate new ideas. Watch how the chef goes about his work – you will learn as much from his methods as from the things that he tells you.

Details of the courses appear in the pages of the magazine. If you have not seen any such holidays advertised, write to the leading women's magazines, such as *Woman, Woman's Realm* and *Woman's Own,* enclosing a stamped addressed envelope, and ask if any courses have been arranged. They are often organised during the off-peak autumn and early spring periods.

Travel companies also arrange cooking holidays, among them Page and Moy of Leicester. For details contact your local travel agent.

## Night Schools and Polytechnic Courses

Private schools and holiday courses can be expensive, but your local authority will probably run a variety of courses on cooking and catering which, though you do have to pay for most of them, will be a lot cheaper. Apply to your local education authority for a list of courses. Most cookery courses start in the autumn.

# 2

# Getting off the Ground

## SETTING UP SHOP

It is perfectly possible to start cooking for money in your kitchen without making very many changes and without purchasing a lot of new equipment. You could do bulk-cooking for a WI market or your local wine bar, or batch-make jams and preserves for a nearby shop; you could probably even get a small-scale dinner party catering service off the ground without too much upheaval.

### Special Equipment

Some jobs are very much easier to carry out on a large scale if you have the right sort of equipment, and even with a small business you will find that you need to buy special items. By far the best approach is to assess at the outset precisely what you are going to need, and then work out how much you can afford to buy straight away and how much you will need to buy later on out of ploughed-back profits. Look at the kitchen check list in chapter 3, if only for future reference.

*'I thought you knew how it worked.'*

A food mixer or food processor would be an essential immediate investment for most home cooking activities, the choice depending largely upon what you are planning to do. A food mixer is ideal for all forms of baking, whereas a food processor takes a lot of the work out of general cooking. It also has the advantage of fewer parts to wash up and store. You will find that an electric carving knife is invaluable for large-scale catering. Special equipment needed for specific activities is covered in the relevant chapters.

If at all possible, find a corner somewhere in your house and use it as the office. An old desk and a small filing cabinet would get you started, but I cannot stress enough how important it is to have a place where you can keep all your records, correspondence and account books, and work undisturbed. If you have a family, try to get them used to the idea that you should be left alone when working at your desk.

## Sources of Information

You will probably already have a good collection of cookery books, but you will find that most of these books do not give recipes for more than four, six or eight people. There are one or two good books on cooking in quantity available in book shops but a look at the catering schools' set lists could prove even more useful. I have, for example, a book called *The Complete Patissier* by William Barker, published by Northwood Publications, which is the definitive book in this area – all the recipes are for twelve plus.

Some manufacturers and growers have clubbed together to provide a general information service, and have produced leaflets for caterers to show how their foods can be used to best advantage. Many of these organisations give recipes for large-scale catering, which can act as guidelines for the conversion of other recipes.

*Possible Sources*
Send a stamped addressed envelope to the following organisations and explain exactly what your requirements are.

The Flour Advisory Service,
10 Doughty Street,
London WC1N 2PL.

The Meat Promotion Executive,
5 St John's Square,
London EC1N 4DE.

The Mushroom Growers' Association,
Agriculture House,
Knightsbridge,
London SW1X 7NJ.

New Zealand Lamb Information Bureau,
The International Business Centre,
29 Glasshouse Street,
London W1R 5RQ.

The Pasta Information Service
(and also the Sausage and Bacon Bureaux),
26 Fitzroy Square,
London W1P 6BT.

The Potato Marketing Board,
50 Hans Crescent,
London SW1X 0NB.

The Rice Information Service,
6th Floor, Hulton House,
161–166 Fleet Street,
London EC4A 2DP.

The Sea Fish Kitchen,
144 Cromwell Road,
London SW7 4EF.

## Insurance

Another important area to consider when you are getting started is the whole question of insurance. The topic may not seem very important if you are only planning a part-time business, but, even so, you may be using your own or your partner's car for delivery purposes and this could affect the insurance on the car. An accident need not necessarily be your fault, but you could be left with a nasty bill to pay because you were not properly covered by your existing policy. Check with your insurance company and make the necessary changes.

Insurance is particularly important if you are thinking about starting a catering operation. You must be covered for claims both from customers and from people who might be working with you. Food poisoning doesn't happen very often, but even the most careful caterer can be sued for causing illness. Waitresses could break an ornament or damage a piece of furniture in your client's home and you could be liable; someone who is working for you could hurt themselves in the kitchen. An insurance policy is essential. Go to see a good insurance broker and he will help you to find a suitable insurance company.

Another area which needs insurance is, of course, the freezer. If you have not bothered with this for personal use, do consider it for the business. You could lose a lot of money if the freezer breaks down when it is full. If you have decided to run a freezer service, then naturally insurance is a must.

You might also consider taking out some health insurance if you have given up a job and are planning to run a full-time business. This policy would bring in an income in the event of long-term illness or permanent ill health.

## Telephone Answering

It goes without saying that to run a small catering business from home you will need to be on the telephone. You should also think about using an answering service or having an answering machine to take messages, inquiries and orders while you are out.

British Telecom approved telephone answering machines can be rented, bought outright or bought over a period of time. But unless you are very careful with your recorded messages a machine can sound rather unfriendly and some people simply will not talk into one. The alternative is to use an answering service. Here, a real person answers the telephone and, in addition to giving any messages you specify, will make sure of getting the caller's name and number so that you can ring back. You can put your own telephone number and that of the service on your stationery and promotional material, or you can have a direct line installed so that calls can be automatically transferred to the second number. Details can be obtained from British Telecom, and under Telephone Answering Services in the Yellow Pages.

## Transport

You are going to need the use of a car or van for most of the money-making activities outlined in this book. You need transport for making deliveries, and for getting yourself, the prepared food, raw ingredients and equipment to the venue.

If you intend to buy a car or van specially for the business, think carefully about your requirements. An estate car, for example, is not such a good idea for a catering business as it might seem at first. The open design means that equipment cannot be left in the car overnight for fear of theft. And it also means that the food is more exposed to the sun that it would be in a car or van.

If you already have a car and plan to use it for transporting food, you must think about the hygiene aspects. Even if the food is well wrapped, you should not use a car in which you regularly carry pets; the boot should be kept really clean and you should not have spare petrol cans or even dirty Wellington boots in it at other times. Most precautions are pure common sense. But, to be on the safe side, have a look at the Food Hygiene (Market Stalls and Delivery Vehicles) Regulations 1966 No 79. (See chapter 3.)

# BUYING IN BULK

As soon as you start cooking food for sale you will find that you are buying items in much larger amounts than you have ever done before. You must consider getting some kind of discount for quantity.

Paper for headed notepaper and invoices, packaging materials and aluminium foil are much cheaper if they are bought in bulk. Other things may be cheaper if you can get a trade rather than a retail price, and you may even be able to negotiate small discounts for quantity at your local shops.

### Buying Food
Your largest outlay is bound to be on food, whether for general catering or for the ingredients for your chosen products. If there is a wholesale cash and carry store in your area, apply to join it.

A wholesale cash and carry is invaluable if you are buying large amounts of the same ingredients – and you can buy your household items at discount too. Such organisations usually want to see some proof that you are in business, and your printed stationery, a selection of promotional material and a letter outlining the type of busi-

ness you are running should get you in. You will be issued with a cash and carry card, and you can, with a banker's reference, arrange a cash limit with the store.

You will also need to use your local shops. This may be a question of convenience (you do not always want to trail off to the cash and carry for a small number of items) or a matter of quality. If you are catering for top-class dinners, you need to be sure of the quality of the meat and vegetables you are serving. Local suppliers will sometimes give discounts on quantities costing over a certain amount or on whole boxes or cartons of food.

Look around the shops in your area to see who is supplying the best produce and then talk to the proprietor about your own operation. Very often he or she will be interested in your venture and be happy to help.

## Packaging

Packaging materials can mount up to quite large sums, particularly if you are making preserves or sweetmeats for sale. There are wholesale cash and carry outlets which sell packaging materials, and some food cash and carry wholesalers stock items like foil, greaseproof paper and paper bags.

There are a number of mail order companies who specialise in packaging. Lakeland Plastics, for example, sell everything that the freezer service operator might need. WI market controllers can usually suggest a good source for the packaging you will need for selling produce at a WI market.

If you are not sure where to buy your packaging materials, buy a copy of *Packaging News and Packaging Today* and have a look at the companies who are advertising. They may be selling just the sort of thing you are looking for. Write to them setting out your requirements, and they will either supply direct or put you in touch with a stockist in your area.

## Stationery and Office Materials

Here again, buying in bulk can save you a lot of money, but you do need the room in which to store such large quantities. A ream of paper costs a lot less per sheet that buying it in batches of fifty or a hundred. Printing costs, too, are such that the more you print at one go, the cheaper each unit will be.

I managed to save quite a tidy sum by having my letterhead printed on my compliment slips and invoices in exactly the same size as on the notepaper. This meant that the printer ran the same artwork for all three items and the cost of printing the compliment slips and invoices was simply a run-on cost rather than the price of new artwork and a second start up. I use the compliment slip as cards and leave them after events and parties or give them to guests who ask for information about London Cooks.

# 3

# How to go about it

## ORGANISING YOUR BUSINESS

The way you choose to organise your business will depend very largely upon how much time you have available and upon the size of the operation you want to run.

It is very important to think ahead. You may not have much spare time now, but you could have more in the future, or the business could go so well that you decide to take on extra help. If this happens, it is a lot easier to expand if you have already taken care of the formal aspect of the company. There are three options open to you: sole proprietorship, partnership and a limited liability company.

### Sole Proprietorship
In this instance you trade on your own and under your own name and there are no legal requirements to be met. However, if you decide to add any extra words to your name, such as Janet Smith Sweetmeats or Brian Jones Catering, or if you are using a completely different name, such as Party Fare or Farmhouse Pantry, then you are affected by the Companies Act 1981.

The Act requires you to disclose the name of the owner and the address at which documents can be served if necessary. This information must be given on all business letters, written orders for the supply of goods or services, invoices and receipts issued in the course of business, and written demands for payments of debts arising in the course of business. You must also display the information prominently so that it can be read easily in any premises where the business is carried on and to which customers or suppliers have access.

In a sole proprietorship claims can be made on your private assets if your business runs into debt.

### Partnership

Having someone else in the business can help to spread both the work load and the worry, but unless you know your partner really well and trust him or her thoroughly it could lead to problems. Each partner is legally responsible for the debts of the business and there is no limitation on this liability – your partner could run off with all the money and you could be left with substantial bills to pay. Even when a partner retires from the partnership he or she may, unless they notify all persons dealing with the firm that they are no longer part of that firm, be liable for debts incurred after their retirement.

If you decide that you need a partner, then make sure that you and your partner agree in advance how the business will be run. It might be an idea to have a legal agreement drawn up by a solicitor, which could set out exactly how the profits are to be split and might even outline areas of responsibility. Arrange with the bank that both parties must sign every business cheque before it becomes valid, and make sure that both partners check and agree the accounts.

There is no need to register a partnership, but if you are using more than the partners' own names as the name of the business or if you are using a completely different name, you will again need to comply with the 1981 Companies Act.

*A Private Limited Liability Company*

The advantage of this arrangement is that the personal financial commitment of the members of the company is limited to their existing investment and in the event of loss they are liable only up to the value of the shares they hold.

There are certain tax advantages to be gained from trading as a limited company. However, if the director's fees are your sole source of income, you will pay income tax on schedule E as an employed person rather than on schedule D as a self-employed person. Forming a limited company affords protection of the company name and confers exclusive rights to the name which no one else may use.

The mechanics of setting up a company are quite easy and may be done through your solicitor or through a company broker.

If you want to get going in a hurry, you can actually buy a company 'off the shelf'. If, however, you want to use a specific name, a search will have to be carried out to ensure that the name is not already being used before the broker will form the company for you. One point to watch is that the Articles of Association are sufficiently wide to take in any activities into which you may wish to expand in the future.

# DEALING WITH THE MONEY

Start by opening a separate bank account and, if you are planning a full-time business, consider getting yourself an accountant. You should also work out a system of detailed accounting records which will still work well if the business really takes off.

You may think that this is all rather unnecessary if you are only planning to spend part of your time in money-making activities, but it is not. You do not want whatever money you make or turn over to get mixed up with your private or joint account, and you must be able to tell whether the venture is paying its way or not. A separate bank account is also a must if you want to pay the taxman no

*'Profit percentage? No, I think it's marrons glacé!'*

more than is absolutely necessary.

Do not expect to pass everything over to an accountant to sort out. Accountants can be expensive, and you still have to supply all the information before they can sort out any muddle you may have made.

## Registering for VAT

Good accounting procedures are essential if you have a major venture in mind. You may be liable for VAT, for example. Remember that, unlike income tax, the VAT base is calculated on the amount of money you *turn over* rather than on the amount you make after paying your expenses.

If you think that you may reach the VAT base fairly quickly, register at once and include the necessary information in your accounting records. Check the current levels with your local VAT office (under Customs and Excise in the telephone directory). The VAT people are usually extremely helpful and will pay you a visit to make sure that you understand what is involved and to give advice on keeping records and making returns.

Depending on the nature of your business, it may be worth making a voluntary registration for VAT even though your turnover is below the base level. This would enable you to re-claim VAT on running expenses, such as petrol, telephone bills and professional fees, and on any initial investment.

## Opening a Bank Account

Open an account either in your own name or in your registered business or company name. In the case of a company you will need to produce your registration certificate along with sample signatures of those partners or directors who are authorised to draw on the account.

Tell your bank manager about your new venture and make any special arrangements which might be necessary. An overdraft facility is usually a good idea so that it is there if a short-term cash flow problem should arise. Your credit rating is important and you do not want to land in a situation where your cheques start to bounce!

## Setting Up Accounting Records

Book-keeping does not need to be complicated. Four sets of accounting records should be sufficient for a large-scale concern, covering payments out of your bank account, payments out of loose or petty cash, invoices sent out to customers and clients, and payments coming in. A small-scale business could manage with only two books: a payments book and a receipt book.

Remember to keep the invoices, receipts and vouchers from all purchases made for the business. If you are registered for VAT, receipts will need to carry a VAT number, and if you are in doubt, ask specifically for a VAT invoice.

### Cash Payments Book

The first set of records concerns all your cheque payments out of your business account. Think carefully about all the expenses you are likely to incur such as ingredients, paper bags, foil containers, pots and pans, letter-headed paper, books and hire of glasses. Arrange the expenses in categories, such as food, packaging, kitchen and office equipment, stationery, research and training, and catering equipment hire. Do not forget to include a section for cheques drawn for your petty cash float.

Buy the widest cash analysis book you can find, and arrange these categories across the top of the columns, leaving three columns for the total amount spent including VAT, the total analysed amount spent excluding VAT, and the VAT amount itself. List the outgoings in date order and total up every three months (to coincide with your VAT returns if you make them).

You will need to start a numbering system which relates payments to invoices, vouchers and receipts. Do not just rely on the cheque number, but number each transaction in the Cash Payments Book and put the same number on the relevant voucher. File the vouchers in order or, if you are using a loose-leaf payments book, place them behind the page on which they are listed.

In a small business this book can be very simple indeed and can include petty cash payments.

### Petty Cash Book

This is the record of all payments not made by cheque. You will need to keep a cash float for immediate payments. In most businesses, these payments usually only involve small sums for postage, petrol and small items of stationery. With a catering business, however, the sums could be much larger. You may do quite a lot of your food shopping from petty cash, and casual staff nearly always want paying in cash.

Keep your Petty Cash Book in just the same way as your Cash Payments Book, but include an additional column for payments in. The categories across the top will also be similar, with an extra column or two for postage etc. Keep the bills wherever possible.

In a small business this book can be combined with the Cash Payments Book.

### *Home Sales Day Book*

This is essentially a record of all the invoices you send out. You don't need a Sales Day Book if all your invoices are kept together in date order. Use pre-numbered invoices and make sure that you keep a copy of each one. If you have had your own invoice paper printed, have it pre-numbered or you will have to remember to type in the number when making out the invoice.

The Home Sales Day Book should list every invoice sent out in number and date order, and should include details of the person and/or company to whom the invoice was sent, the total amount excluding VAT and the VAT amount (if applicable).

Your accountant may suggest that you include the terms of payment on the invoice, such as 'Cash on Delivery', 'Strictly 30 days net' or '2½% Discount for settlement under 20 days'. Remember to cost the latter into your price as you may be taken up on it! Remember also to include in the Sales Day Book a column for the date of settlement. As long as this remains empty it will act as a reminder to chase the customer for payment. It will also enable you to check the length of the payment time, which could be important when assessing the value of certain customers in the future.

Total the Home Sales Day Book monthly to see how much money is outstanding, and keep the copies of the actual invoices in a loose leaf file as a double check. Transfer invoices to a different section on payment.

If a lot of supplies are bought on credit, it may be helpful to have a *Purchase Day Book*. This would show the date of purchase, the supplier, the invoice amount, VAT if applicable, a reference to a purchase order or requisition if used, discounts available for prompt payment and the date of eventual settlement. The Purchase Day Book can often be kept in the same book as the Sales Day Book.

## Cash Receipts Book

This is the complete record of all the money that comes into the business, whether it is paid in cash or by cheque, or, indeed, whether you have paid it in yourself as a loan to the business.

The way you set out this book will depend upon the kind of analysis you may want to make as your business progresses. If, for example, you start off with a mixed activity business such as baking, jam making and country produce, you will probably want to know how much of your income comes from each source. Of, if you are running a catering business, you may want to know the difference in income between large-scale buffet parties, business luncheons and children's parties. These records will help you to assess the profitability of the various sections of your business.

The example set out below includes a bank column, in which are listed the payments into the bank from the paying-in book. These are reconciled against the receipts listed daily. The column for 'other receipts' will include capital introduced, bank and building society interest, commission and so on.

### Cash Receipts Book

| Date | | Received from | Total Amount | | Preserves Sales | | Baking Sales | | Country Foods Sales | | Other | | V.A.T. | | Bank | |
|------|---|---------------|-------------|---|-----------------|---|--------------|---|---------------------|---|-------|---|--------|---|------|---|
| March | 7 | A. E. Black | 86 | 25 | 75 | 00 | | | | | | | 11 | 25 | | |
| | 8 | Capital introduced | 200 | 00 | | | | | | | 200 | 00 | | | 286 | 25 |
| | 27 | Grapes Wine Bar Ltd. | 287 | 50 | | | | | 250 | 00 | | | 37 | 50 | 287 | 50 |

## Other Records

For some types of business, a book of goods loaned and hired might be very useful to help reconcile hire bills and deposit charges.

# GETTING IT RIGHT

As soon as you start working from home you are regarded as self-employed and become liable for national insurance contributions and income tax. Your culinary activities will also be affected by a variety of government regulations covering hygiene, labelling, packaging and composition of food.

Once you have decided what you are going to do, go and talk to you local Department of Health and Social Security Office and buy copies of the relevant legislation from Her Majesty's Stationery Office shops.

## National Insurance

You should notify your local DHSS office of your self-employed status as soon as you sell your first item of home produce or do your first job for a customer. The DHSS publishes two leaflects (NI 41 and NI 27A) which give full information on national insurance contributions for the self-employed. They are very useful indeed and they can be obtained free from any DHSS office. Self-employed people pay Class 2 national insurance contributions.

If you earn less than a certain amount you may not have to pay any national insurance contributions, but to achieve this exemption you must apply for, and be granted, an exemption certificate. Your local DHSS office will be able to tell you what this exemption level is and how to calculate it. If you are not sure how much you are going to make, you can apply for deferment, but this should be done before the beginning of the tax year in which the contributions will be payable. If you think that you might qualify for exemption, it is wise to consider your position very carefully; you could lose benefit in the future, and if you have been paying national insurance contributions in the past you may lose the advantage of these.

Some married women and widows have the right to reduced national insurance liability, and if you qualify you should have a certificate of election. As long as your certificate remains current you can continue to pay Class 1 contributions at a reduced rate. Incidentally, these certificates were issued prior to 1978, since when the option has been removed.

If you do well and the profits from your business exceed a certain limit, you will have to pay Class 4 contributions as well as Class 2. These are earnings-related and are worked out as a percentage of your profits liable to tax under Schedule D. The upper and lower limits for Class 4 contributions are usually updated each year.

If your business starts to grow to the extent that you need to take on outside help, make sure that your helpers are registered as self-employed or that their earnings are below the liability level for national insurance employment contributions, otherwise you will find yourself paying employer's contributions.

## Income Tax

From the moment you take your first payment you will become liable for income tax. Income tax is assessed on your net income or profit, which is the amount of money you have left after paying all your costs and expenses. To find out how much you can earn before becoming liable to tax, check with your local tax office or accountant.

If you are self-employed, there are all sorts of expenses which you can charge against your income, but the rules are very complex indeed. Generally speaking, you can charge expenses which are 'wholly and exclusively incurred in the course of business'. These include items such as ingredients, packaging, postage, stationery, advertising, petrol, delivery costs and cooking, waiting and secretarial help. Less obvious are special work clothes and overalls, research material such as recipe books and magazines, training courses and your accountant's fees. Make sure that all of these are fully analysed in your Cash Payments Book.

You may also be able to claim a percentage of the running costs of your home and car against tax. These items could include rent, rates, insurance, telephone charges, heating, lighting and cleaning in respect of rooms used wholly or partly for the business, and car maintenance. It is a good plan to put regular expense claims through the accounts for reimbursement. Back up records, in the form of a note of hours of use for the cooker, a record of telephone calls and delivery mileage for petrol, will help considerably in getting the correct percentage agreed with the tax man.

# FOOD LEGISLATION

The Food and Drugs Act 1955 and the subsequent Food Act 1984 contain a vast body of legislation referring to all aspects of the preparation, composition, packaging and labelling, and sale of food. They are the 'umbrella' acts for all the regulations referred to later in this section. You become liable to the provision of the act the moment you make food for sale. The section of the Food and Drugs Act 1955 which is immediately relevant is Section 16, and this requires you to register with your local authority. In practice, this usually means contacting the local Department of Environmental Health. The Health Inspector will probably want to inspect your kitchen to see that it conforms to the provisions set out in the Food Hygiene (General) Regulations 1970 No 1172. The inspectors are usually most helpful and more than willing to advise on the health and hygiene aspects of your proposed business.

## Food Hygiene Regulations

Whether you are making and selling food direct to the public, selling through another retail outlet such as a shop or a café, catering for dinners and parties, or, indeed, engaging in any of the activities mentioned in this book, you should read and understand the provisions of the Food Hygiene (General) Regulations 1970 No 1172.

These Regulations contain general requirements for the cleanliness of premises used to prepare food for sale, the hygienic handling of that food and the cleanliness of the people involved in the

preparation of the food. They are enforced by the local authority, usually by the Environmental Health Department. Some authorities issue their own detailed guidelines, which prove extremely useful, particularly if you need to make some changes to your kitchen.

The Regulations require the premises where food is handled (your kitchen) to be well ventilated and to have nothing about their situation or construction which might lead to contamination of food by dirt, germs, insects, vermin or odour. You will need to be sure that the floors and walls of your kitchen can be easily cleaned down and that there is no unnecessary woodwork or panelling which could harbour dust or insects. You may also need to install a canopy over your cooker and an air fan in the window.

The Regulations also state that, where unprepared food is handled, there should be enough sinks for washing both the food and the equipment used. This will almost certainly mean that the Public Health Inspector will want to see a double sink unit in your kitchen.

Waste disposal is another important point. You must not store rubbish in your kitchen or allow too large an accumulation of rubbish anywhere on the premises.

If you have so much work that you need to use outside help, the Regulations can make things even more complicated by requiring the provision of sanitary and washing facilities, first aid kits and clothing lockers.

Another very important point to remember when using outside help is that you are not allowed to send food out for preparation or packing in someone else's home. If you have large batches of food to pack you must get your helpers to come to your kitchen.

Here is a check list of all the things you should consider about your kitchen before setting up in business. The list may look a bit formidable, but the chances are that as long as your business remains very small you will not be required to make very many changes. However, it is sensible to know what might be required in the future and to budget accordingly.

**Kitchen Check List**

| | |
|---|---|
| *Ceiling* | Easily cleanable |
| *Walls* | Easily cleanable with no unnecessary woodwork or panelling to harbour dust or vermin |
| *Floor* | Made of durable, impervious material, easily cleanable |
| *Ventilation* | Kitchen ventilator |
| | Canopy over the cooker |
| *Lighting* | Minimum of 20 lumens per square foot at working level |
| *Workspace* | Sufficient work tops for everyone likely to be working in the kitchen; the tops should be non-absorbent and washable |
| *Washing facilities* | Double sink unit |
| | Washbasin and sanitary arrangements downstairs |
| *Equipment* | Movable for cleaning and unlikely to harbour dust or vermin |
| *Storage* | Adequate fridge and freezer space |
| | Adequate ventilation in larder |
| | Hanging space for staff's outdoor clothing |
| *Refuse storage* | Adequate space and containers |

Other sections of the Regulations refer to the cleanliness of everyone taking part in the preparation and handling of the food. Here the recommendations include frequent washing of hands while engaged in cooking, wearing special clothing or overalls, wearing waterproof bandages on open cuts and, of course, no smoking. It is a good idea to change aprons, tea towels and dish cloths each day and to boil these when they are washed. Most caterers that I talked to said that they were much more careful in the kitchen now than they had been before setting up in business.

Food which has been prepared and is waiting to be packed or delivered must be properly screened and shrink wrap is the answer here. Foods which contain meat, game, poultry, fish, gravy and artificial cream must not be kept between the temperature of 50°F/10°C and 145°F/62.7°C. They must be kept really hot or really cold. Serious outbreaks of food poisoning have occurred because food has been left for several hours at lukewarm temperatures at which germs multiply most easily.

Other general points to watch include keeping any family pets well away from the kitchen, and this means that their food should be stored in a different place from that stored for human consumption. Also, if anyone in your family or among your helpers contracts an infectious disease or has any kind of typhoid or salmonella or staphylococcal food poisoning, you must inform your local medical officer of health at once.

The Food Hygiene Regulations have the full backing of the law and anybody who does not keep them properly can be prosecuted. Penalties range from a fine to three months' imprisonment.

## Composition of Food

Some foods such as jams and preserves, sausages, meat pies, tomato ketchup and cheese have certain standards of composition laid down by law. Any homemade produce which you are planning to sell and which falls into one of these categories must conform to these standards. You can buy copies of the relevant food orders form an HMSO bookshop or through an independent bookseller. Some of the orders and regulations you may need to refer to are given below.

No 589 Food Standards Fish Cakes Order 1950
No 691 Food Standards (Preserves) Order 1953
No 1307 Food Standards (Preserves) (Amendment) Order 1953
No 1817 Food Standards (Tomato Ketchup) Order 1949
No 1167 Food Standards (Tomato Ketchup) (Amendment) Regulations 1956
No 1304 The Bread and Flour Regulations 1984
No 94 The Cheese Regulations 1970
No 1122 and 649 The Cheese (Amendment) Regulations 1974 and 1984
No 927 The Fruit Juice and Fruit Nectars Regulations 1977
No 1311 The Fruit Juice and Fruit Nectars (Amendment) Regulations 1984
No 1832 The Honey Regulations 1980
No 1566 The Meat Products and Spreadable Fish Products Regulations 1984
No 541 The Cocoa and Chocolate Products Regulations 1976
No 17 Cocoa and Chocolate Products (Amendment) Regulation 1982

This list is by no means exhaustive and new orders, regulations and amendments are introduced from time to time. So check with the Ministry of Agriculture, Fisheries and Food, Food Standards Division, Great Westminster House, Horseferry Road, London SW1P ZAE (Tel: 01–216 7253) to see whether or not there is any legislation covering the foods you are planning to make, or whether any of the regulations have been superseded.

A further piece of legislation which you may need to refer to if you are planning to add any preservatives to your produce is No

1834 The Miscellaneous Additives in Food Regulations 1980. These and the No 14 Miscellaneous Additives in Food (Amendment) Regulations 1982 and the No 752 The Preservatives in Food Regulations 1979 and Amendments 1980 and 1982 set out permitted additives and prescribe the way in which food containing these additives should be labelled.

## Labelling of Food

Food made with preservatives or other additives is not the only food to be governed by detailed labelling legislation. The Food Labelling Regulations 1984 No 1305 require all food for sale to be marked with the name of the food, a list of ingredients, the name and address of the business, an indication of how long it will last, any special storage requirements, and instructions for use if it would be difficult to use the product without these instructions.

These Regulations need to be read in conjunction with the food orders and regulations listed in the previous section and the Weights and Measures Act 1979 and Amendments 1980/82/84.

Here are some points to watch when you are labelling your products, but do read the Regulations for yourself as well.

### Name of the Food
The name used to describe your product must be precise enough to inform the buyer of its exact nature. If there is a customary name for the food in your area, or a name prescribed by law, then this name must be used. If you think up an attractive name for your product you may use this *with* a more precise name. For example, you may want to call your marmalade 'Farmhouse Breakfast' or your buns 'Fairy Angels'. If so, they must be labelled as 'Farmhouse Breakfast Marmalade' or 'Fairy Angel Buns'. On the other hand, Lemon Cheese and Sally Lunn are customary names and will not need additional descriptions.

### List of Ingredients
This list must be headed by the word ingredients. All the ingredients must be included and they must be listed in descending order

of weight as determined at the time they were weighed for use in the preparation of the food. Even water must usually be included in the list of ingredients.

The Regulations give a list of generic names which may be used for ingredients, such as cheese, flour, oil, nuts and sugar, together with details of how these names may need to be modified. Oil, for example, must be accompanied by the description animal or vegetable, or, if appropriate, by the specific origin of the oil, such as sunflower seed oil.

### Name and Address of Maker
The details given here must be sufficient for the producer to be contacted through the postal system.

### Indication of the Life of the Product
The minimum durability of your product must be indicated by the words 'best before' followed by the date up to and including that on which the food can reasonably be expected to retain its quality if stored properly. This should be followed by details of storage conditions which may need to be followed if the food is to last until that date.

If the product is a perishable food which is intended for consumption within six weeks, the words 'best before' may be replaced by 'sell by'.

Until January 1985 any food with a minimum durability of 12 months does not need to include any indication of durability. After that date the minimum durability is 18 months for all foods.

This section of the Regulations does not apply to frozen food or to foods which are expected to last for more than 12 months. (After January 1 1985, the figure is increased to 18 months.)

### Legibility
All the information you are required to give must be clearly visible on or through the packaging. It must be easy to read and easy to understand.

*Claims and Misleading Statements*

The Regulations go on to cover claims about dietary foods and misleading statements about the contents of the product. For example, you may not use the word butter, or any other word which implies that biscuits contain butter, unless at least half the fat used is milk fat. The Trade Descriptions Act also limits the claims that you can make about your products. If you simply state the truth you should be all right.

## Licence for the Sale of Alcohol

A licence from HM Customs and Excise is required for the sale of wholesale quantities of wines and spirits. This means that if you are asked to supply more than a case of wine for a luncheon or maybe a full bar for a party, you will need to have a licence. This can be obtained by filling in a short form and paying a small fee. The forms are obtainable, together with an explanatory leaflet, from your local Customs and Excise office – addresses and telephone numbers in the telephone directory.

# 4

# Selling Yourself and Your Product

## WHO WILL BUY?

Successful selling depends, first, upon identifying your outlets and, second, upon knowing as much as possible about the requirements of those outlets. You need to know what sort of products or services people are looking for, at what price and so on.

The answer to the question 'who will buy' depends partly upon the products or services you are offering and partly upon the answers to the market research questions outlined in chapter 1.

For some activities, the outlets will overlap. Once you have decided which are the most likely to fit in with your plans, you will need to study them in more detail. A summary of outlets and a few basic points to consider are given here; more information on specialist activities is given in the relevant chapters.

*Direct Sales to the Public*
- Is there a WI market in the area and, if so, what specialities does it have?
- Is there an open or closed market or a street market nearby, and what are your chances of joining it?

**Summary of Main Outlets**

| Outlet | Activity | Outlet | Activity |
|---|---|---|---|
| Direct sales to the public via market and roadside stalls | Baking<br>Home preserves<br>Country foods | Direct sales to the public to order | Cake decorating<br>Freezer service<br>Lunch boxes and picnics<br>Dinner parties<br>Large-scale catering |
| Indirect sales through retail outlets such as shops and tea rooms | Baking<br>Home preserves<br>Country foods<br>Sweetmeats<br>Frozen foods | Mail order | Sweetmeats<br>Country foods*<br>Home preserves* |
| Indirect sales through catering establishments such as restaurants, pubs and wine bars | Sweetmeats<br>Country foods<br>General cookery | | |

*Limited by the safe life of the food and the problem of breakage in transit.

- Are there any competitive products being sold on the market, or is there a gap to fill?
- Do you own the land immediately adjacent to the road by your house which would be suitable for a roadside stall?

*Indirect Sales through Retail Outlets*
- Have you checked all the possible outlets in the area?
- Are there any competitive products being sold, or is there a gap to fill?

- Can you make out a case why selling your products will benefit the retailer?
- Is there likely to be sufficient display space, and what is the retailer's mark-up likely to be?

### Indirect Sales through Catering Establishments

● Have you checked all the possible establishments in the area?
● What sort of food do they offer? Is there room for improvement or for a totally different kind of food?
● Can you make out a case why offering your food will benefit the establishment?
● What is the mark-up likely to be?

### Direct Sales to the Public to Order

● Have you thought about the life style, needs and tastes of the local community?
● Is there any competition, and what is it doing? Is there an obvious gap?
● Make a list of all the different categories of potential customers who may be interested in your services?

### Mail Order

● Will the product stand up to (rough) handling in transit?
● Will transport costs put the price up too much?
● Do you think people will want your products enough to send off for them?

## BRINGING IN THE BUSINESS

You should now be in a good position to decide whom to approach in order to sell your product or service. So how are you going to make contact with potential outlets?

The first method is, if course, by direct contact with the customer at the market or roadside stall, and more of this in chapter 5. The second method of making contact is by post, and this may mean either sending individual letters to the proprietors of local shops and catering establishments or organising a large-scale mailing to potential customers for a dinner party or large-scale catering service. The third method is by advertising, and this method could be useful for any of the activities you choose to pursue.

## Personal Letters

Writing a personal letter to the proprietor of your target outlet is really only the beginning. It is the way to get his or her interest and must be followed by a personal visit, when you can really concentrate on putting over the advantages of your product. This initial letter is very important. It should be designed to sound interesting and intriguing (you want to ensure that the recipients will agree to see you), but it also needs to be professional in approach. Do not sound too mysterious or go on for too long. On the other hand, you must not give so little information that the recipient is unable to see in your proposition any advantage for himself or his business. You must sound as though you know what you are talking about – and if you have done your market research properly you will!

*Sample letter to a local retailer*

> Dear Mr Merryweather,
>
> I am writing to see if you would be interested in discussing the possibility of selling my range of homemade toffee and fudge.
>
> I notice that you already offer a number of items of local interest for sale, though you do not have any sweets. My toffee and fudge are both made to traditional recipes using local produce, and the range is packed extremely attractively.
>
> I feel sure that the addition of this range can only add to the business already attracted from the increasing number of tourists in the area.

I would like to call in to see you one afternoon next week and look forward to hearing which date would be most convenient for you.

Yours sincerely,

Such a letter has a personal approach – the owner is addressed by name. The product on offer is named and some of its advantages outlined with reference to existing business. *Do not be too modest here; if you are not enthusiastic about the product, who will be?* The sales opportunities have been touched on and you have ended with a definite request for a meeting.

If you do not get a reply within a few days, follow up with a telephone call to finalise the date for a meeting. When you get to the meeting have with you all the facts and figures needed to back up your statements. And do not forget to take samples! If the proprietor is really interested, you will then be able to discuss prices, quantities and delivery dates.

A letter to a local catering establishment would follow along the same lines, giving details of the sort of food you might provide and why you believe it would benefit the landlord or wine bar proprietor to put it on the menu. You might also point out what the opposition is doing and show how business might be attracted away.

## Direct Mail

Another way of attracting business and getting yourself and your venture known is to write a large number of letters to potential customers. Start by looking at your lists of types of potential customers and the services they might be interested in and choose those targets which you think would be likely to yield the most business.

You might have noticed, for example, that weddings are extremely frequent at the local churches, or that there are a large number of businesses in the area that may need outside catering on a small scale. Write a letter setting out details of the services you have to offer and enclose any promotional leaflets you have had printed. The letter should be short and to the point.

## Sample letters

Dear Miss Taylor,

Congratulations on your engagement to James Smith.

I specialise in making and decorating wedding cakes and would be delighted to have the opportunity of quoting for your own cake.

I enclose details of my services and would be happy to show you photographs of some of the lovely cakes I have made.

I look forward to hearing from you.

Yours sincerely,

or

Dear Mr Swinburn,

My company specialises in catering for all kinds of business functions, from small luncheon buffets to full-scale office parties. We aim for interesting menus made from quality foods at sensible prices.

I enclose some sample menus to give you a taste of our service, though we would be equally delighted to devise menus specially for you.

Please give me a ring any time.

Yours sincerely,

Depending on the numbers involved, letters can be individually typed or typed once and photocopied. Whichever method you choose, do try to keep the mailing as personal as possible. Never write to the 'Managing Director' or the 'Public Relations Manager' – always type in the name and address of the recipient.

The names and addresses for these mailings could be compiled from announcements in the local papers, advertisements in the Yellow Pages or in the local paper, or from personal knowledge of the area. The mailing does not necessarily have to go through the post; it can be dropped straight into people's letterboxes.

## Advertising

The choice of where and how to advertise will depend on whom you are trying to sell to. The question to ask is 'What sort of newspapers or magazines are my potential customers likely to read?' And do not forget about the Yellow Pages and shop windows.

Wherever you decide to advertise, the general principle is the same: try and make your advertisement stand out from the others. This can be done by adroit wording and by the use of arresting type faces or attractive drawings. Very often the sales representative from the publication or directory will be able to help you with your wording and design.

## National Newspapers and Magazines

Advertising in national newspapers and magazines can be a costly business, but it is well worth considering if you are thinking of a mail order operation where you need to spread the net as wide as possible. Study the advertisements in various papers and magazines to see which are most likely to be useful to you. If you do not have too much money to spend, the personal columns might prove a better bet than a display advertisement.

Obviously, if your business is very local in nature, then advertising in a national publication would be a waste of time, but if the publication only goes to people who are likely to be interested, then the reaction could be quite good. A London cook specialising in high-class dinner parties, for example, regularly advertises in *The Tatler* and *Harpers & Queen*.

## Local Newspapers and Magazines

Here, the chances of your advertisement being seen by someone who needs your services and lives within the area you serve are very much better, and, of course, the rates are much cheaper.

Some newspapers gather together all the advertisements relating to a particular activity and this increases the possibility of interest being shown in your advertisement. Your local paper may have a weekly wedding half page or feature a particular topic supported by related advertising.

Advertising your products or services in local county magazines is well worth considering; they concentrate on leisure and social activities and are usually taken by those who have a little extra money to spend.

## *Local Radio*

There are more than thirty local radio stations scattered across Britain and they offer another useful advertising medium. Don't try to be too clever with your advertisment: stick to the point and simply describe your services and the way that they can help to enhance the listener's life style.

## *Yellow Pages and Local Directories*

The advantages of directory advertising is that it is localised. The Yellow Pages own advertising campaign has ensured that people are aware of the directories and their use. One disadvantage is that to be listed in the Yellow Pages you need to have a business telephone connection and the rental for this is higher than for a private line.

Be wary when dealing with directories other than Yellow Pages. There have been a number of cases in the past of so-called directory operators taking money for advertisements in their directories and then only printing and distributing a few copies. Before committing yourself, make sure that the directory is going to be properly distributed.

## *Shop Windows and Notice Boards*

If your business is small-scale and local in its operation, shop window notice boards could be very useful. Make sure that you have an attractive design on your card, or at least that it is neatly typed, and it is bound to stand out from the rather tatty collection of advertisements found on such boards. The main attraction of this method is that the cost is very low.

A source of free advertising might be the notice boards of local companies. The more your goods or services are likely to be needed by the company's employees, the more likely they are to put your advertisement up. Write to the personnel officer by name, and keep your advertisement small and neat. It certainly will not go up if it takes up the whole board!

# HOW MUCH TO CHARGE?

One of the first things that potential customers will want to know about your products or service is the price. It is important to try and get this right at the very beginning . If you pitch your prices too high you will not bring in the business, and if you pitch them too low you will have difficulty in raising them to a proper level. Customers quickly become accustomed to low price levels and will resent anything more than general cost increases.

So where do you start? It is impossible to give actual price examples because costs and conditions vary so much in different parts of the country, and a menu which would be reasonable in London, would horrify customers in Lancashire or Lincolnshire. Similarly, if you have access to a seaside fish market or can buy direct from the boats, the input to your home smoking business will be much cheaper than it would be elsewhere.

By all means, start by having a look at the competition's prices, but do not try to undercut just for the sake of it. You can compete just as well with better products or menus and first-class service, or by offering to deliver free of charge.

The next step is to make a list of *all* the items which are likely to be involved in making your product or in producing your service. Make sure that you have not forgotten anything. Very small items, such as salt and pepper or sticky labels tend to get left out, yet the cost of them can mount up over a period of time. Don't forget to include the cost of fuel and any extra help.

Then take a sample quantity of, say, 25 or 50 products and estimate the cost of each item on the list. Try to be as accurate as possible here. The total of this column will give you an *initial cost* for the product. However, it does not take into account all the other costs or overheads (such as advertising, stationery, telephone and postage) that you will incur as part of running your business. You must therefore try and estimate the cost of overheads. Divide the monthly overhead figure by the number of products or services you hope to make or provide during a month and add a percentage amount to your initial product cost.

Headings which might appear on your cost calculation sheet are as follows:

*Initial costs*
Ingredients, broken down in as much detail as possible
Fuel costs, gas and electricity
Packaging and containers
Labels
Wrapping materials
Delivery costs
Staff costs

*Additional or overhead costs*
Stationery
Advertising
Promotional literature
Cost of running business premises
Research material
Training
Work clothes
Provision for replacement costs

Many people stop at this point and use this product cost as the basis for the price by simply adding a 100% or 200% mark-up, depending on what the market will bear. The trouble with this approach is that the mark-up may not cover your *own* time. Are you earning as much as you would be if you were working for the same amount of time outside the home? Nor does this method of costing take into account the cost of capital equipment such as cookers, freezers, small electrical appliances, or a stock of crockery and serving dishes.

It is particularly important in the early stages to check your estimated costs against real costs, and to adjust your prices as soon as you find any discrepencies.

# PRESENTING YOUR PRODUCT OR SERVICE

The first thing that people will see or hear about your business is its name, and it is worth giving some thought to what you are going to call yourself. You can, of course, use your own name; if you are well known locally and your business is likely to be limited to that area, then making use of your own name is probably a good idea. A personal name can also convey an image of homemade goodness.

## Choosing a Name

Your own name may not mean very much to the majority of people in your catchment area and you may want to look for an attractive name which conveys, perhaps, the flavour of what you are offering. I believe that for certain types of business, such as a catering service, a business name projects a more professional image. In the early days, it can also help to make your business appear more substantial and experienced than it is!

If you do decide to use a business name, choose one that is memorable. This usually means one that is not too long and not too esoteric. Check in the local telephone directory or Yellow Pages that none of the names you think of is being used locally, and pick the one that you feel best conveys the essence of your business. You will have to give, by law, the full name and address of the proprietor on all your business stationery.

You may want to go one step further and to think of names for each of your products. In this case, check with the legislation referred to in chapter 3 regarding the labelling of produce.

## Packaging and Labelling

The second thing that customers see is your product, and market research shows that the appearance of a product is very high on the list of factors which influence a customer's choice. The choice of packaging is therefore very important; not only should the packaging look good, it must also do its job in terms of protecting the product from the elements and from damage. It is no good having a really attractive bag to hold your toffees if the edges of the sweets are likely to tear the paper.

Labelling, too, needs careful consideration. It must be legible by law and you want the customer to get all the information he can. Make sure that the names are prominent and easy to read. A fancy type face may be attractive to look at but hopelessly difficult to read. You could always achieve a memorable impact, not by the lettering, which must be small, but by the use of a logo or drawing. A logo could be derived from the initial letters of your business name; a drawing could depict your name or your product.

## Presentation

Do not slip into the trap of thinking that if you are offering a service rather than a range of products you do not need to be concerned about how your efforts are packaged. The way in which you present your buffet table, dinner menu or decorated birthday cake

is just as important to the success of your business as the shape of the jars or the design of the labels are to a home preserving business.

I spoke to one young cook who had just completed her first six months in her own catering business. She confessed that the one thing she had not thought about in advance was the presentation of her food. Lots of watercress was the sum total of her first attempt at garnish. But after looking at the way in which dishes are presented for photography in glossy cookery books and magazines, she now comes up with some really mouthwatering displays.

# BUILDING A REPUTATION

The better known you and your products become, the better it will be for your business. If potential customers have heard your name before or read about you in the local paper, they will be much more receptive when you approach them for business or when they see your products on sale. The reaction, 'Oh, I've heard of them', is usually a reassuring thought to a potential buyer.

There are a number of things you can do to try and build up an awareness of your home cooking activities. Your local paper may be interested in doing a story on you when you first start up, and if you are clever you may be able to get them to do follow-up stories whenever you do something of particular local interest. The local radio station might also be persuaded to interview you, and if this works well they could always invite you back to do a longer talk or perhaps even a phone-in.

Get to know the local reporters. See if you can get a mention when the wedding reception you have just catered for is written up, or when you have produced a spectacular or an unusually-shaped cake. Take a photograph and, as well as adding the picture to your records, send it to the local paper.

When you first start up, it is an excellent idea to write to the features editor of your local paper by name along the following lines.

Start off by introducing your subject as follows: 'I am writing to tell you about a range of products/service which I have recently introduced to the Reading area.' The next paragraph should outline the details of your service, concentrating on anything that you think is different to other similar businesses. If you or your partner has changed jobs or life style to accommodate the new business, this information should also be included. Your last paragraph should offer to provide more information, either through a telephone conversation or through a meeting.

You may wish to follow up your letter with an invitation to sample the range of products or, if you are catering for lunches, dinners or parties, with an invitation to lunch.

Some of the companies in your area may be large enough to produce their own house magazine and you may be able to get the editor to feature your activities, particularly if you have provided something for a company event or for a member of staff.

Depending upon the range and scope of your business and where you are situated, you may also want to write to the features editor of suitable national magazines. Generally, these people will only be really interested if you are offering a product or service which is out of the ordinary or which is topical for some reason.

Quite a few of a the national home interest magazines, such as *Good Housekeeping, Home and Freezer Digest* and *Homes and Gardens,* run shopping columns and once you have got your range of products well established in a number of different outlets you might consider sending a press release to the editors of these columns.

A press release is quite easy to write. Stick to the facts and write them out in a clear and logical fashion with the most interesting points first. Use your letter-headed paper and type the words PRESS RELEASE in capitals at the top. Follow this with a headline outlining the contents of the release.

This simple press release was devised for the very successful Jean Pierre Depesme of Jean Pierre's Pantry Ltd, and it will act as a guide.

## PRESS RELEASE

### New Range of Home Frozen Foods on Sale in London

A new range of home frozen foods made by Jean Pierre's Pantry Ltd of 65 Queenstown Road, London SW8 3 RG went on sale in March this year.

Sold under the Pantryman brand name, the range includes a choice of starters, main courses and desserts which are suitable both for quick family meals and for simple entertaining. Dishes include Watercress Soup, Smoked Haddock Mousse, Navarin of Lamb, Veal Marengo, Beef Bourgignon, Cottage Pie, Chocolate Mousse and French sorbets. Costs range from 90p for the soups to £3 for the Veal Marengo.

The Pantryman range of frozen foods is a development of the very successful dinner party service run by Jean Pierre over the last three years.

Everything is prepared, cooked and frozen on the premises and only the finest and freshest ingredients are used. The dishes are all packed in single portion packs which makes them particularly useful for people living alone.

Orders can be placed by telephone and collected between 11.00 a.m and 6.00 p.m. Monday to Friday and 10.00 a.m. to 1.00 p.m. Saturday. Orders over £50.00 can be delivered free of charge in the Central London area.

Plans are in hand to distribute the Pantryman range through specialist grocers and department stores.

ENDS

A press release should be accompanied by any printed literature that you may have. There is no need to include a covering letter unless you feel that an invitation to sample the food would be a good idea. Don't expect masses of coverage immediately; successful press relations is the result of sustained contact over a period of time.

Another form of name promotion is your own car or van. You can have thick PVC notice printed which can be stuck to the door panels and then removed at a later date – they can have quite an impact but they are not cheap. Other promotion ideas include give-aways such as matchboxes, drinks mats or biros with the name of your business printed on them. These can also be expensive and their effect can only be long term. If you are in catering you might consider having your own label wines.

By far the most valuable recommendation that any enterprise can have is by word of mouth. All the ideas outlined above can help to get you talked about, but if every satisfied customer recommended you to someone else you would have orders enough. Your own high standard of produce and service is really the best Public Relations help you can have.

Create a good impression from the start and aim at doing everything you can that will help people to remember your name and to return to you again and again. Follow up inquiries at once. Send out sample menus the day they are requested. Deliver when you say you will, and arrive with plenty of time to spare for catering functions. Maintain a consistently high quality and give a consistently good service and you will not have any problem in building up a reputation and in bringing in the business.

# 5

# Baking for Market Stalls

Perhaps the simplest way to start cooking for money is to sell home-baked produce at one of the many Women's Institute markets. These markets are run in church or village halls and the stalls are organised for you. Though you are expected to take an active part in the market, you do not have to go out and sell your products in quite the same way as you would on the open market. However, the profit margins are relatively low and once you have gained some experience you may want to go it alone and start up your own market stall.

## FINDING A MARKET STALL

### Joining a WI Market

A full list of all the markets run by the WI can be obtained by writing to the National Federation of Women's Institutes, Markets Department, 39 Eccleston Street, London SW1W 9NT, enclosing a stamped addressed envelope. The list will tell you if there is a market near where you live. You will only have to make the journey

once a week, but the cost of the petrol will have to be deducted from the money you make.

The next step is to ask the Markets Department to give you the name and address of your local market organiser, and then to make arrangements to go along and talk to her. She will be able to tell you how the market operates, what sort of goods sell well and whether there are any obvious gaps in the produce regularly on sale, how to price your own baking and what sort of initial outlay you should expect to make.

You do not need to be a member of the WI to join a market; buying a 5p share in the market gives you membership. The markets usually operate once a week and are run by a committee elected by the shareholders. They, too, do not need to be members of the WI but must be members of the market.

All shareholders are entitled to sell goods at the market, and are also expected to help out occasionally with the general running of it. It is a good idea to volunteer to help with the running of the stalls as this is very good experience for running your own stall at a later date.

The market organisers to whom I spoke all said that they welcomed younger cooks at their markets. Their general complaint was that so many younger women either went out to work and did not have the time to cook for the market or only cooked convenience foods. So if you are good at making pastry, bread or popular foods such as pizzas and quiches you should be welcomed with open arms.

The WI produces an invaluable handbook, also available from 39 Eccleston Street. It is entitled *Pleasure and Profit from a WI Market*. Write for a price list and then send for the book enclosing a cheque or postal order. The book department at the WI seems to turn orders round very quickly.

## Setting Up Your Own Market Stall

Setting up your own market stall is rather more difficult than joining a WI market and, in some areas, may be almost impossible in the short term. In my own area of Kensington, the waiting list for one street market is ten years and for others five years. The situation is almost as bad elsewhere in the country.

Broadly speaking, anyone who wishes to sell anything from a stationary position on the public highway can only do so if he or she holds a licence. Licences are usually issued annually by the local council. The rates vary depending on the area and on the number of days the market operates.

The first thing to do is to contact the market manager through the council offices and he will tell you how long the waiting list is and how to go about getting a licence. The licence fee and weekly or daily charges are for the use of the site only, and traders are responsible for all other arrangements, such as the hire of the stall, electricity supply and so on.

In addition to public markets there are also private markets on private property. Here you have to negotiate a rent with the owner or organiser. These can be very expensive and may even be a cover for criminal activities, so check the credentials of the owner and the method of operation very carefully!

# RULES AND REGULATIONS

In addition to any rules and regulations imposed by the local council or by the market organisers, you are bound by the government legislation in chapter 3. As well as the Food Hygiene (General) Regulations which cover the preparation of food at home, there are the Food Hygiene (Markets, Stalls and Delivery Vehicles) Regulations 1966 No 791 and the Amendment to those Regulations No 1487. These Regulations cover the cleanliness and hygiene of the presentation and handling of the food on the stall and include provision for all stalls selling open or unwrapped food to be adequately covered and screened. You are also required to display the name and address of the stallholder.

Remember, too, to check on the relevant packaging and labelling regulations and the weights and measures regulations and the Trade Descriptions Act. In the case of WI markets, the WI handbooks and the market controller will tell you how best to comply with the various regulations.

# WHAT TO MAKE

WI markets and market stalls are not limited to the sale of home-baked produce – they also sell home preserves, country foods and sweetmeats. However, these subjects are covered in later chapters and this section concentrates solely on home-baked produce.

The choice of what to bake is pretty wide, but whatever you decide to make do use good ingredients. These will not necessarily be the most expensive, but you must always aim to produce a good homemade result. This is important both for the reputation of a WI market and for your own reputation in any type of market. Let the family eat up the slightly overcooked cake or the broken pastry flan.

## Bread

Bread is always a popular item, and wholemeal bread sells particularly well. Under the Bread and Flour Regulations 1984 No 1304, bread must be made in strict accordance with weight regulations. Fruit and malt loaves are considered to be flour confectionery and are not included in these regulations.

To be sure of making a 400g loaf, begin by weighing out 454g of dough and adjust this quantity for subsequent loaves if the finished loaf does not weigh 400g. Keep to the same recipe and always weigh out the ingredients carefully.

## Cakes, Buns and Biscuits

This kind of homemade food is always popular. Sponge cakes, sandwich cakes and fruit cakes disappear quickly. All cakes should be well and evenly cooked and attractively finished with sugar, butter icing or regular icing. Cake mixes should not be used and nor should eggs which have been bought broken out of their shells. If you use artificial cream rather than real cream in any cakes, a notice must be displayed to inform customers of this fact.

Traditional cakes and biscuits are popular, and so are small cakes and buns which can be bought by single people. Small cakes are a good choice as far as the producer is concerned as more money can be made on these than on large cakes. Biscuits and cookies can also be sold singly or in small packs of four, six or eight.

## Sweet Pies and Pastries

Sweet pies go down well, and here again they should be well and evenly cooked and nicely finished off round the edges, perhaps with a simple leaf pattern on the top. However, one market organiser laughingly suggested that they should not look too perfect or customers would not believe that they were really home-baked!

### Savouries

*Twice cooked meat must never be used in savouries.* This means that you cannot use any bits of leftover meat in Shepherds Pie or in pasties. If you are selling savouries you must display a notice saying 'These articles contain no preservatives. KEEP COLD and consume as soon as possible'.

Mcat pies and sausage rolls are covered by specific regulations: No 1566 (see chapter 3). These are mainly concerned with the amount of meat in pies. A homemade meat pie or sausage roll will probably have more than the required amount of meat, so don't skimp and you will keep within the regulations and keep your customers at the same time. Make sure that all these items are well cooked, and cool them as rapidly as possible after taking them out of the oven.

### Puddings

Steamed puddings and Christmas puddings make good winter lines. Cook them carefully – you do not want your customers to complain of soggy puddings.

*In no circumstances should you make the produce in advance and freeze it.* It is illegal to sell food which has been frozen and thawed before being sold. It is, however, quite permissible to freeze pies before they are cooked and bake them freshly for the market.

## Which Ones for You?

What you decide to make will depend upon your own skills, upon what is likely to sell and upon what other people are selling. Try to choose things that you like making because you will be producing them in much larger numbers than usual. It is an advantage if you are used to batch baking for your family freezer.

If you are going to join a WI market, take your list of items to the market controller and be guided by her; she has the experience to know what is likely to sell and what will not. Concentrate to start with on two or three lines and do them regularly. It will take a few weeks to see if they are 'taking', but if they do, stick to them. A lot of market customers like to place regular orders for specific items, so if you do decide to drop one item and do something different one week, check first that the market organiser does not have advance orders.

Once you have been with the market for a while you may decide to branch out. Most market organisers will tell you that it is very much a matter of luck as to whether something a little out of the ordinary goes well or not. Make sure it looks attractive and persevere with it for at least three or four weeks before passing judgement on its sales potential.

If you are going to run your own market stall, you will need more lines and the decision will have to be made on your own. Do some market research. See what other food stalls in the market are doing. Look at the local cake shops and go along to the WI market, if there is one, to see what they are selling. It is probably best to have a range of tried and trusted items like sandwich cakes, fruit cakes, tea loaves, chocolate buns, shortbread and ginger biscuits, and then try out some more unusual items alongside. As in the WI market, you will have to keep new items running for a few weeks before taking a decision on whether to retain them or not.

## Ideas for New Lines

Even though the WI market is a co-operative and you will not want to compete with other producers on a cost basis or by producing the same items, you do want to make some money and one way of doing this is to stand out in some way. This is even more important in a public market where you are very definitely competing with everyone else. Some successful new lines could be one way to be noticed – along with a consistently high standard of cooking and good ingredients. Check that no one else has thought of them and try them out.

### Regional Specialities

These nearly all sell well so do some research and see what your area has to offer. Here are some ideas to set you off:

| | |
|---|---|
| *Saffron Cake* | Cornwall |
| *Sally Lunn* | West Country |
| *Eccles Cakes* | Lancashire |
| *Maids of Honour* | Home Counties |
| *Shrewsbury Biscuits* | Shropshire |
| *Lardy Cake* | Wiltshire, Oxfordshire, Gloucestershire |
| *Teacakes* | Yorkshire |
| *Bakewell Tart* | Derbyshire |
| *Ormskirk Gingerbread* | Lancashire |
| *Cheesecakes* | Leicestershire |
| *Parkin Cake* | Yorkshire |
| *Apple Cake* | Somerset |

Very often these specialities sell just as well out of their own areas!

### Seasonal Specialities

There are quite a lot of baked foods which are traditionally served at special times of the year.

| | |
|---|---|
| *Christmas* | Cakes, Mince Pies, puddings |
| *Easter* | Simnel Cake, Easter Biscuits, Hot Cross Buns, Fig Pie |
| *All Souls Day* | Soul Cakes |
| *New Year* | Coventry God Cakes |

You could also create special cakes to a theme. Examples would be

Bonfire Cakes for Guy Fawkes Night, Witches Hats (buns) for Hallowe'en and heart-shaped cakes, buns or biscuits for St Valentine's Day.

*Your Own Specialities*
All good cooks have their own specialities which family and friends are always asking for. Very often they are variations on a popular theme, such as feather-iced cakes, flavoured shortbread or cheese or oatmeal scones. Or they may be something quite different concocted by yourself or from an old family recipe book. If your foods are popular with the people you know, try them out in the market.

Other ideas can come from commercial sources. Have you noticed anything which has come into the shops recently and which seems to be selling well? If you have, try out your own version on the market buyers. Pizza is one food which has gained in popularity over the last few years; and Passion Cake is another more recent addition to the delicatessen counter.

# PACKAGING AND LABELLING

There are very few statutory regulations for the packaging and labelling of cakes and flour confectionery such as buns, sweet tarts and biscuits, but they must be adequately protected from any kind of contamination.

The WI markets suggest window bags with transparent fronts and greaseproof backs, and these are ideal for most things. Polythene bags can be used for sticky foods, but not for decorated cakes where they might stick to, and thus remove, the icing. Here, a cardboard base and a side collar encircling the cake will be necessary. The whole lot is then placed in a window bag. This is a much better method of showing off the cake than in a cake box, which can also be very expensive.

Staples should never be used to close bags as these are dangerous for children and blind people. Use a little sellotape to seal. Pack small items as tightly as possible to prevent damage. A piece of card in the base of the bag will help to protect the food and stop grease spots appearing on the paper back of the bag.

Bags, card bases, collars etc can usually be bought through the market, or the market organiser will give you a list of suppliers. For those who are thinking of setting up their own stalls, some addresses are given in the Appendix.

Sweet pies and savoury produce can be cooked and sold in foil containers, which makes them much easier to handle. Puddings can be made in foil basins with a vinyl coating, to avoid perforation.

The labelling and contents of some savoury foods are affected by The Meat Products and Spreadable Fish Products Regulations (see chapter 3), and you should also refer to the regulations concerning packaging and labelling if you make puddings for sale.

WI markets produce self-adhesive labels suitable for use with various kinds of products and these should be used for everything that you cook for the market, including those items which are not covered by the statutory regulations. You should give the name of the cake, biscuit or pie, together with details of flavourings and fillings. For example, Orange Sandwich Cake with Orange Butter Filling. The same system would be sensible for items sold on your own stall. Remember to give your name and address for extra orders, and do not use margarine in butter icing or you will be contravening the Trade Descriptions Act.

# STARTING UP

Once you have agreed with your market organiser what you are going to do, you will need to invest in some packaging materials, spend some money on the first few batches of ingredients and perhaps buy some more baking tins. An average starting-up cost when joining a WI market is £30. As it gets used up, replace this amount from profits and you will always have a little working capital in hand.

If you do decide to go out and buy more baking equipment, remember that rectangular tins make more economic use of oven space than round ones. If you are making items which need to have the tins lined, cut out a piece of greaseproof paper to the correct size and make a cardboard pattern. Thereafter you can use the pattern as a guide which will save you having to measure up every time you bake – quite a consideration if you are lining oval or other odd shapes.

Obviously, the outlay is going to be much greater if you are setting up your own stall; quantities will be much larger and, of course, you will need to buy or hire the stall itself. Do not buy too much equipment to start with. You may find that you change your lines early on and some of the new equipment will be redundant.

Display material for your stall is important. You will need cloths which will look attractive but wear well. And if you can vary the height of the display area by using blocks or tins under your cloths, you will be able to set out a much more eye-catching display than you could on a flat surface.

Make sure that customers realise that all the produce is home-made, and where appropriate use signs to point out the use of fresh cream and butter. Remember that such claims must be true.

If you want to produce goods in larger quantities but are unable to find a market site, think about selling through cake shops, delicatessens, cafés or craft shops. Your local health food shop could be interested in selling a range of pies, cakes and biscuits. Interest in vegetarian and whole-foods is very much on the increase and good ready-prepared food is not always easy to find.

## HOW MUCH TO CHARGE

The WI markets have their own methods of pricing. You need to keep a record of the cost of all the ingredients for each item baked. Do this costing very carefully. If you use you own home-grown items such as fruit or eggs, cost them in at the price at which similar goods are selling in the shops. Then add in the cost of the packaging.

The next step is to add one third of the total cost of ingredients and packaging into the first total. This is to cover fuel and time.

Finally, add on one third of the second total for profit.

Every time you take food to the market you will need to submit an invoice, together with a copy invoice. (Use a proper invoice book, *not* scraps of paper, as this adds to the work of the treasurer and may lead to mistakes.) One copy of each invoice is returned to you at the end of the month, together with a record of any returns and a cheque for the amount you have made. The market charges a small fee for expenses, which amounts to about 10–15%.

If you are planning to set up your own stall, you will probably need to charge more as your overheads are going to be quite a lot larger. Have a look at the section on pricing in chapter 4 and work out some sample prices, then see how these compare with other stalls or with the prices charged in confectionery shops. Do not be too depressed if your prices come out higher. Provided that your produce is of a consistently high standard, shoppers are usually prepared to pay a premium for homemade produce.

## GETTING YOUR NAME KNOWN

At the WI market your produce will, if it is popular, become associated with your name and regular customers will ask the controller for repeat orders.

However, if you are competing on the open market rather more effort is required and it is well worth thinking of a good name for your business. Thus, if customers like your produce they have a memorable name to talk to their friends about, and also to give them the confidence to try other lines. Ideas for names can be found in your own name, the name of your house or that of your village or town. For example, Kathy's Kitchen, Sunnyridge Products, Micheldean Home Produce.

# 6

# Making Preserves for Sale

Homemade preserves are always popular and many good cooks are maximising their skills in this area. The market is a round-the-year one but with a peak at Christmas and , if you live in a tourist area, another one in the summer.

## WHAT TO MAKE

The choice includes jams, jellies, marmalades, chutneys, pickles and fruits in alcohol. Your own skills and preferences will help you to choose exactly what to make. Some items like raspberry and strawberry jam are always popular, but, because of the individual nature of the market, unusual specialities can also sell very well indeed.

Take a look at the following list. Add in your own favourite recipes or experiment to produce a new flavour combination.

*Jams and Jellies*
Use fruit with a high pectin content to ensure a good set, or choose combinations of fruit to overcome any possible setting problems.

*'I think we'll give blackberry preserve a miss next year.'*

Apples, redcurrants and gooseberries are all useful for adding to fruit with a low pectin level. Mixing different fruits together can make for some delicious flavour combinations.

*Jams*
    Apricot with Almonds
    Gooseberry with Elderflowers
    Marrow Ginger
    Strawberry and Gooseberry
    Cherry and Redcurrant
    Damson and Pear
    Rhubarb and Ginger
    Plum or Greengage Conserve with Raisins and Citrus Fruits
    Quince or Mulberry
    Melon and Lemon Preserve

*Jellies*
>   Bramble
>   Cranberry
>   Rowenberry
>   Elderberry and Apple
>   Crab Apple
>   Bilberry and Apple
>   Spiced Redcurrant
>   Quince
>   Sloe and Apple
>   Strawberry and Redcurrant

## Fruit Curds and Butters

Fruit curds are creamy fruit mixtures made with fresh fruit, eggs, butter and sugar. Lemon curd is probably the best known of these.

Fruit butters are very thick mixtures of fresh fruit pulp and sugar. The preserve gets its thickness from the concentration of the fruit and the sugar. Large quantities of fruit are required to make fruit butters and so they are usually only made in times of glut.

*Curds*
>   Blackberry and Apple
>   Orange and Lemon
>   Gooseberry and Ginger
>   Apricot and Lemon

*Butters*
>   Plum and Apple
>   Spiced Apple
>   Blackcurrant and Walnut
>   Rhubarb, Raisin and Ginger

## Marmalades

Although Seville oranges are only available in the late winter months, marmalade can be made all the year round from sweet oranges, grapefruit and other citrus fruits. They can range in texture from thick and chunky to a very smooth clear jelly. Fruit mixtures also produce very good marmalades.

Orange, Lemon and Grapefruit
Seville Orange, Ginger and Apple
Lemon and Lime Jelly
Grapefruit and Tangerine
Pineapple and Lemon

### Fruits in Alcohol

Preserving fruit in alcohol can produce an expensive product. However, the results are delicious and ideal for Christmas presents. Mincemeat also falls into this category, though the amount of alcohol included is not sufficient to keep the product for more than a few weeks.

Apricots in Brandy
Peaches in White Rum
Cherries in Whisky
Pears in Port Wine
Raspberries in Brandy
Victoria Plums in Orange Liqueur

### Chutneys

The list of possible combinations of fruit and vegetables for chutneys is almost endless. Most people have their own tried and tested recipes, some of which have been handed down for generations. Here are few of my favourites.

Spiced Apricot and Orange
Rhubarb, Raisin and Onion
Green Tomato and Onion
Damson and Apple
Onion, Apple and Date
Banana, Raisin and Ginger
Marrow and Tomato

Pear and Orange
Spiced Pineapple
Plum and Carrot

*Pickles*
Beetroot, onion and red cabbage are probably the joint favourites in this category but, here again, unusual homemade pickles can find a niche for themselves. And do not forget that fruit also pickles very well.

Beetroot and Horseradish
Apple and Pepper Pickle
Pickled Peaches
Spiced Pears
Piccalilly

Some people make and sell all kinds of preserves, making those which are appropriate to the produce available at particular times of the year. Others prefer to specialise in, say, jams or chutneys and to freeze produce in plentiful supply at one time of the year for use at another.

There is, indeed, a lot to be said for specialising to start with. You will be able to perfect both your recipes and your preparation techniques and customers will get to know your products and to ask for them by name. One supplier of chutney, operating from her Norfolk home, offers a range of just six chutneys, yet they sell to people all over the country and also abroad. Her perfected recipes are a closely guarded secret, except to the Weights and Measures people!

# GETTING IT RIGHT

There are very stringent statutory requirements governing the production of preserves and you must be very careful not to fall foul of these. First of all, your kitchen must conform to the Food Hygiene

(General) Regulations 1970 No 1172 covered in chapter 3.

There are specific orders and regulations relating to the composition, packaging and labelling of produce and these are listed in chapter 3. You should also consult the Weights and Measures Acts 1963, 1976 and 1979 which contain valuable information.

There are some major points to watch in several categories of home preserves.

## Jams, Jellies and Marmalades

Preserves which are on sale to the public must have the correct soluble solid content. This refers to the proportion of sugar to fruit and means that in no circumstances should more than 10 lb of jam be obtained from 6 lb of sugar, irrespective of the amount of fruit used. This is the finished weight when weighed in the pan.

To be sure of getting the correct soluble solid content you should follow the principles of preservation given in the official Ministry of Agriculture publication, Bulletin 21, 'Home Preservation of Fruit and Vegetables'. The Bulletin includes recipes for all kinds of preserves but there is no reason why you should not convert your own recipes provided that you keep within the regulations.

Always fill your jars to the top. Under the Weights and Measures Act, jam must be sold by minimum weight in prescribed quantities of 2 oz (57g), 4 oz (113g), 8 oz (227g), 16 oz (454g) or a multiple of 454g. To ensure that you get the correct amount into the jar use standard 1 lb and ½ lb jars.

## Fruit Curd and Mincemeat

These preserves are also affected by the soluble solids regulations. Tested recipes may be found in the Ministry of Agriculture's Bulletin 21. If you have a favourite recipe that you want to use, you may be able to persuade your local Weights and Measures Authority to test it for you.

Fruit curd and mincemeat do not have to be sold in prescribed amounts. However, 1 lb and ½ lb jars should be marked 14 oz (395g) net and 7 oz (198g) net respectively because with these preserves it is sometimes impossible to ensure that the full 16 oz and 8 oz weight gets into the jars.

### Chutneys and Pickles

The content regulations for chutneys and pickles are not quite so stringent as for jams and marmalades. However, you should make sure of using a good quality vinegar with a minimum acetic acid content of 5%, and never dilute the vinegar with water.

Chutneys and pickles should not be sold until they have matured for two months. Red cabbage is the only exception as it loses its crispness after a few weeks.

The weight labelling of chutneys and pickles is also much easier than for other preserves. They are labelled by fluid measure and a 1 lb jam jar holds 12 fl oz (341ml), regardless of what is in it.

# PRESENTING YOUR PRODUCE

Jars, tops and labels are very important both in terms of ensuring the correct life of the product and in presenting an attractive appearance. Needless to add, they are covered by legislation.

## Jars and Tops

Despite the temptation to use an attractively shaped jar, it is probably sensible to go for standard clear jars. You will then be quite sure that the fluid content is correct. The sizes chosen could depend upon the products you choose to make, but 1 lb and ½ lb are the most popular sizes.

Never use a jar which bears a trade mark or, indeed, any mark which will associate it with any known commercial brand. Always make sure that jars are sterilised and clean, taking particular care with the threads of jars which take twist tops. (A second-hand boiler could be a great help here.) All tops should be new. Second-hand tops may not give a proper seal.

Jam, jellies, marmalades and fruit butters can be covered with metal twist-off tops, polythene tops or cellulose covers and wax discs. Lemon curd should only be covered with a wax disc and a cellulose cover as it does not reach a sufficiently high temperature during preparation to allow the safe use of twist-off or polythene tops.

When using twist-off or polythene caps, make sure that the preserve is potted when it is still close to boiling point. Fill the jars to the brim and put the top on immediately. With polythene tops, it is a good idea to pair them with the jars beforehand to ensure a tight fit. Never use wax discs under either of these kinds of tops.

When using cellulose covers and wax discs, apply the wax disc immediately the jam is potted. The cellulose cover can then be put on at once or the pots can be covered with a cloth and left to go completely cold before the cellulose cover is added.

Chutneys and pickles should be covered with twist-tops, polythene or metal lug tops. A ceresin disc will be required with metal lug tops to keep the vinegar away from the metal.

An attractive 'country' touch can be given to jars of preserves by covering the tops with small circles of check or floral cloth. These are added after the proper seals have been applied and are usually held in place by rubber bands. Colour code the different preserves or match the material to the design on your labels.

## Labels

All labels for preserves must include the following details: name of the preserve, list of ingredients, name and address of maker, net weight in imperial with metric equivalents, indication of durability, instructions for storage, any preservatives or additives, and the price. Design your labels so that there is enough room to give the required details.

### The name of the preserve
This must be precise enough to inform the purchaser of the true nature of the product he or she is buying. See page 42, chapter 3.

## List of Ingredients

See page 42, chapter 3, for details of the regulations. You must mention even the smallest quantity flavourings. However, you do not have to give away your flavouring secrets. If you have used more than one spice you may simply include these as mixed spices, and any kind of orange, lemon, lime or grapefruit peel may go in as citrus peel. Raisins, sultanas and currants can be specified as vine fruits. But if you have used nuts in the recipe, these must be specified unless they make up a quantity of less than 1% of the total.

## Name and Address

See page 43, chapter 3.

## Net Weight

Jams, jellies and marmalades must be sold in the prescribed amounts given on page 80 and should be marked as such. Statutory prescribed metric amounts will eventually take the place of prescribed imperial amounts. Lemon curd and mincemeat should be marked with a minimum net weight in both imperial and metric and chutneys and pickles with the fluid weights also in imperial and metric.

## Indication of Durability

See page 43, chapter 3.

## Instructions for Storage

See page 43, chapter 3. The labels for items such as Pickled Red Cabbage should include the words 'best before' followed by a date up to which time the food can reasonably be expected to retain its specific properties. Any storage conditions necessary should also be stated, for example 'Refrigerate on opening'.

## Preservatives and Additives

Many producers like to reinforce the homemade aspects of their products by stating that there are no preservatives or additives in their produce.

*The Price*
The regulations require that the selling price is given on the labels of preserve.

As well as being informative, labels are also the only point of contact that you are likely to have with your end customer and so they must project the right image. It is certainly worth calling in a professional designer to advise on the use of drawings, pictures and symbols and to suggest some type faces. The designer should be able to arrange things so that the label is attractive and there is plenty or room for all the information which must be included.

# WHERE TO SELL

There are dozens of different outlets for home-produced preserves. They can start with your own doorstep and end with Macy's in New York! (And that was the true progression for one small brand.)

In the early days when you are not sure how much you can produce and are generally feeling your way, local outlets are probably the most sensible. You could put up a notice saying 'Jam for Sale' and quite literally sell from your own doorstep. However, you must own the land on which you set up the notice or any stall, and in some areas there are rules and regulations stating how near to the road a notice or stall may be. Check with the local council first.

If you live on a tourist route you could sell quite a lot of produce by the roadside, but you will probably be better off selling your products in an environment where people are expecting to buy such things, such as at a market or in the high street. One answer would be to join the local WI market if there is one, and details of this are given in chapter 5. Alternatively you could put your name down for a market stall, but you will still need to look for other sales outlets while you are waiting for it!

So what are the chances in the high street? The answer is quite good. Start by walking round all the shopping streets in your area and jotting down details of the shops you think might be interested. The list will probably include some or all of the following:

### Specialist Grocers

Look out for the sort of grocer who sells the more expensive ranges of products. Very often the words 'High Class' will appear as part of his low-key advertising. Shops which have a good delicatessen counter are also worth noting. Many of these shops sell homemade preserves in addition to their normal lines.

### Cake Shops and Sweet Shops

Do not be put off if these shops are not selling preserves at the moment. There is a good chance that you will be able to convince the owner or manager that you are offering another good profit centre.

### Craft Shops

Shops which specialise in selling local crafts such as weaving or pottery will sometimes consider selling other types of homemade produce. At Totnes in Devon, the Dartington Farm Foods shop specialises in crafts and home-produced foods. However such shops are few and far between so you might even consider setting one up yourself.

### Tourist Shops

Tourist shops take many forms but if you live in a tourist area you will be able to recognise them immediately. They are in the business of selling keepsakes and mementos and your local produce could well come under this heading, particularly if you have borrowed a local name to use as a brand or trade name.

### Cafés, Teashops and Restaurants

Many of these establishments sell local produce as well as serving food, and if you are in a tourist area the turnover of such produce could be very high.

Having made your list of outlets, put them in order of likely sales and write to the top two or three along the lines set out in chapter 4. *Do remember to point out the benefits to them of selling your produce* – you are not asking for favours but offering to add to their profit margins!

Later, you may want to look further afield for your sales outlets. This may mean taking on extra help to deal with large or rushed orders and you will also have to deliver the produce, which will cut into profits. Large city department stores, for example, sell home preserves, some of them all the year round, others just at Christmas time. Approach the buyer for the food departments, or the buyer whose job it is to set up Christmas food fairs etc. Ring up the store to get the names of these people and then write with full details of your products.

## Pricing Your Preserves

Start by reading the section on pricing in chapter 4, then work out your costs using the following headings:

    Ingredients – down to the tiniest amount of spices
    Fuel
    Jars, tops and covers
    Labels
    Delivery costs – including transport and boxes
    Promotional costs
    Other overheads – stationery, telephone and office costs
    Time – your time
    Profit

The final price will depend upon your outlets. The retailer must also make a profit and he is going to add a mark-up. If your price is too high, this mark-up will take the retail price beyond that which potential customers are prepared to pay.

# BUILDING A REPUTATION

Building up a reputation in a business such as this works on two fronts. There is your reputation with the owner or manager of your sales outlet and there is the ennd customer. Obviously the two are interlinked, but they do have different requirements. Your product must be good enough to sell without resulting in complaints from customers but the retailer is really more concerned with your ability to deliver in the quantities required, on time, and with the right sort of promotional back-up. The customer, on the other hand, is looking for an attractive product with consistent quality.

Read the section on promotion in chapter 4. Your retailer will certainly be pleased if you achieve a write-up in the paper that mentions where to buy the products.

Other potential ideas include attaching a small leaflet to each jar containing information about other items in the range. If customers like the items they buy, this approach could bring them back to try some of the others.

The best way to build up a solid and lasting reputation is by the quality of your produce. Make sure that you always use ingredients which are at their peak; windfalls and old fruit just will not do for commercial production. Never cut corners in the processing; a few extra minutes or even an hour is not worth cloudy jelly or runny jam. And once you have worked out a good recipe, stick to it.

# 7

# Selling Country Foods

Meat pies and sausage rolls can be classed as country foods but there are many other traditional meat products such as raised pies and sausages which could be offered for sale. Most of these foods are popular but require a degree of knowledge and skill which is beyond that of most people. If you are skilled in this area you could find a ready market for your products.

## WHAT TO MAKE

The final decision on what to make must rest on an assessment of your own skills, the availability of raw materials and a bit of sensible market research. Here is a list of some of the possibilities with variations on each theme. Add your own specialities to the list.

*Raised Pies and Pastry Work*
Hot raised pastry makes very attractive looking pies which can be made to look even more decorative if they are made in interesting shapes with a little pastry work on the top. Popular fillings are veal and ham, and pork, but one pastry cook I talked to was very

encouraging about the idea of trying out new and different fillings. Her comment was that people liked to be tempted, and out of her range of six the plain pork pie was the least popular. Ideas for raised pies include:

*Huntsman's*
  Chicken and pâté layers
*Traditional*
  Veal, pork and egg pie
*Humble*
  Sausagemeat base with onion or tomato
*Game*
  Chicken, wood pigeon and rabbit terrine
*Pork Special*
  Pork with apple or sage and onion

*Mixed Meat*
    Pork and chicken or pork and beef
*Farmhouse*
    Chicken, bacon and egg

Homemade pies made with puff and shortcrust pastry can also find a ready sale. Use foil trays or flan dishes so that they can be kept with the pie. Individual sizes go well in retirement areas. Try the following:

*Savoury*
    Meat Pie (beef), Meat and Potato Pie, Cornish Pasties, Sausage Rolls, Bacon and Egg Pie, Quiches
*Sweet*
    Gooseberry and Ginger Plate Pie, Apple and Blackberry (and other flavourings), Plum or Damson Pie, Treacle Tart, Blackcurrant Plate Pie, Bakewell Tart

*Sausages*

The important point to remember with sausages is that the texture is as important as the flavour, so separate the fat from the lean and chop each to get the desired effect. On the whole coarse sausages are preferred to smooth ones and pork is the favourite base. However, as with pies, it is worth experimenting a little:

*Cottage Pork*
    Pork with bacon
*Herby*
    Pork with sage, mixed herbs and thyme
*Tomato*
    Pork or pork and beef with tomato purée
*Apple*
    Pork and apple
*Beef*
    Beef with a little lamb fat

*Scottish*
   Liver and oatmeal base
*Cumberland*
   Continuous pork sausage
*Cottage Luncheon*
   Continuous large sausage

The type of sausage skins used can affect the end result and natural sausage skins can be obtained from Gysin & Hanson Ltd, 227–231 Rotherhythe Road, London SE16 2BA.

## Pâtés, Terrines and Potted Meats

Pâtés and terrines sell very well. They do not look quite as neat and tidy as the commercially produced ones, but they are free from preservatives and, indeed, any kind of additive and are very popular because of it.

To make these foods look appetising, use a solid butter topping for extra keeping properties, and things like bay leaves, gherkins, stuffed olive slices and black peppers to make an attractive pattern on the top. These can be set in place with a little aspic. Some terrines are encased in thin rashers of stretched bacon and can be turned out and sliced, or the terrine can be wrapped in pastry with a decorative leaf pattern on the top. Consider making a few of the following pâtés and terrines.

*Herb Terrine*
   Pork, ham, bacon, spinach and mixed herbs
*Duck Terrine*
   Duck, veal and pork flavoured with orange or juniper berries
*Chicken Terrine*
   Chicken and ham
*Game Pâté*
   Wood pigeon or rabbit with veal, pork and brandy
*Venison Pâté*
   Venison with pork and redcurrants

*Chicken Liver Pâté*
  Chicken liver with onion or chopped hard-boiled eggs
*Smoked Fish Pâté*
  Smoked trout, mackerel, salmon or haddock
*Liver Pâté*
  Liver and bacon with a little pork and herbs
*Country Pâté*
  Coarse pork with a little liver and herbs
*Potted Beef*
  Beef with anchovies
*Brawn*
  Pig's head and cheek with herbs or sherry
*Ham in Jelly*
  Ham set in aspic with parsley or other herbs

## Smoked Foods

A smoke house in the garden is a real possibility, particularly if you also live near one of the newly flourishing fish farms. You can smoke meat as well as fish, but in both cases great care needs to be taken with the temperature control.

Most foods need to be lightly salted before smoking. They then go into the smoke house for periods varying from a few hours to a few days. Fish, for example, must be smoked continuously and this can mean getting up to stoke the firebox at regular intervals through the night. Possible candidates for smoking include salmon and trout among the freshwater fish, and haddock, plaice and mackerel if you live near a fishing port. Meats include breast of chicken or turkey, sausages and hams.

## Cheese

If you live in the country, you may have access to large quantities of cows' or goats' milk, or, indeed, you may keep your own animals. If so, the home-produced cheese or yogurt market could be your goal.

Most recipes for simple hard cheese start off with 3 gallons or more of milk and cheese-making could be a very viable proposition if you live on a farm. There are several cheeses that you could make.

>Cottage Cheese, plain or flavoured
>Pressed Cottage Cheese, wrapped in muslin, pressed in an embossed mould or wrapped in vine or other suitable leaves
>Coulommier Cheese
>Neufchâtel Cheese
>Yogurt or Cream Cheese
>Smallholder's Cheese (a semi-hard cheese)
>Colby Cheese, plain or with caraway seeds, sage or cumin seed
>Ricotta Cheese (using up the whey)
>Scottish Blanc (very, very soft cheese)

Goat's cheese and goat's yogurt are further possibilities. Apart from the fact that the 1980 Food Labelling Regulations require goat produce to be labelled as such, the general cheese regulations do not apply to it. There are no regulations covering yogurt, though the yogurt manufacturers' trade association is currently working on a Code of Practice for members.

## GETTING IT RIGHT

### The Regulations

The regulations covering most of the produce discussed in this chapter are fairly extensive. Start by reading the section on the Food Hygiene (General) Regulations in chapter 3 and get hold of the relevant leaflets covering the regulations on your chosen foods.

*Raised Pies, Meat Pies, Sausage Rolls, Sausages, Pâtés, Terrines and Potted Meats*

No 1566 The Meat Products and Spreadable Fish Products Regulations 1984

These regulations are mainly concerned with the amount of meat and fish contained in pies, pâtés etc. It is unlikely that homemade produce would have less than the minimum amounts laid down in the regulations but it will be important to check the levels in the legislation, and to make sure that you do not pad out your pies and pâtés with other ingredients.

*Twice cooked meat should never be used in any kind of meat product,* so do not try to use up any meat left over from an earlier batch of cooking. *Nor should any of your produce be frozen and then thawed before it is sold.* It is illegal to sell food which has been frozen in any other state than frozen.

The temperatures at which you work with or store meat and meat products are very important in order to prevent spoilage. These temperatures are laid down in the Food Hygiene (General) Regulations. Make sure that you cool your produce as quickly as possible after cooking and that you do not leave it lying about in the kitchen before putting it into cool storage.

## Cheese

No 94 The Cheese Regulations 1970
No 1122 The Cheese (Amendment) Regulations 1974
No 649 The Cheese (Amendment) Regulations 1984
No 1833 The Emulsifiers and Stabilisers in Food Regulations 1980
No 2086 The Colouring Matter in Food (Amendment) Regulations 1976

These regulations cover the composition, description, labelling and advertising of cheese. They also cover the permitted additives and colours. Read them carefully as they are quite complicated. All these regulations should be read in conjunction with regulation No 1305 The Food Labelling Regulations 1984.

*Smoked Foods*

Provided that you do not add anything to the items to be smoked, there are no regulations covering smoked fish or meat.

## The Equipment

It is very important to have the right equipment. A large family-size mixer or food processor may be sufficient to start you off making pies, sausages and pâtés, but you will soon need to think about a commercial machine and greater oven space. After all, most ovens will only take two large pies side by side, and even if you have a convection oven the number of pies that can be cooked at once will only be four or five. There will also be a great deal of chopping and mincing to be done and specialised equipment will be very important.

You will probably need to invest in special moulds for raised pies and containers for other types of produce. Some suppliers sell large, cheap earthenware dishes specially made for selling pâté and terrine. Foil containers can also be used.

Specialist equipment is equally important for smoking and for cheese-making. A properly constructed smoker with a reliable temperature gauge is a must for both hot and cold smoking; moulds, followers, cheese press and grids and trays will be needed for cheese-making.

## Presentation

Much of the produce covered in this section will be sold unwrapped or, if it is wrapped, it is likely to be in see-through packaging of some kind. This means that much of the presentation lies in the produce itself. Decorative finishes and patterns will be just as important as the appearance of the packaging and labelling.

Read the notes on the packaging and labelling regulations listed in chapter 3.

# WHERE TO SELL

There are all sorts of outlets which might be interested in country produce. Have a look round your area and try any of the following:

## Markets
Meat products and cheeses can be sold through WI markets or on your own market stall. You will not be able to sell yogurt at the WI market because, as the WI *Markets Handbook* puts it, 'without sterile conditions it is very easy to start up the growth of an unwanted organism'.

Even if you do not have your own market stall, you may be able to persuade a local butcher, specialist grocer or cheese seller with a stall to sell your produce.

## High Street Shops
Some butchers have a wider range of foods on sale than just raw meat, and a tie-up with a butcher could also mean access to a commercial mincing machine or sausage maker. A butcher could be interested in selling your raised pies, meat pies, sausages, pâtés and terrines.

Specialist grocers and delicatessens are excellent outlets for meat products and cheeses. One cook I came across had an informal arrangement with her local delicatessen whereby she supplied all the pies and pâtés for the ready-made food counter and the shop took orders for her produce and helped her to finance commercial equipment. Another similar shop had its own production kitchen on the premises and allowed its resident baker to use the facilities to make produce for other outlets.

Department stores in large towns and cities could also be interested in home-cooked produce and it is certainly worth a letter to the meat products or cheese buyer to see if they would be interested. Remember, though, that the quantities required by such outlets could be quite substantial. Be sure that you can cope before accepting orders. Delivery costs must be taken into account.

## Catering Establishments
Wine bars, pubs and even restaurants could also be interested in country produce. Have a look at chapter 10 for ideas.

# 8

# Sweetmeats for Sale

Some very famous names in the confectionery business started out from their back kitchen, and there is no reason why history should not repeat itself!

## WHAT TO MAKE

Start by making those things that you are good at making and that you enjoy making. Use your basic recipe and experiment with different flavourings and coatings until you have a small but viable range of sweetmeats. Later, if you want to branch out into something different, have a look in the shops and talk to people who are selling confectionery to see what they find sells well.

### Toffee
Homemade toffee is very popular, particularly in the winter. It can be flavoured with chocolate, nuts or spices and the basic ingredients can be varied to give treacle- or honey-flavoured toffee. In addition, the full range of toffees takes in soft chewy Russian

caramels, rolled-up coconut caramels, honeycomb toffee and nut brittle of various kinds.

## Fudge

This is another favourite with countless variations: chocolate, coffee, vanilla, nut, caramel and butterscotch; fruit flavours like orange, lemon, pineapple and raisin. A lovely fudge I came across recently had been created specially for the Christmas trade. It was snowy white in colour and packed full of candied fruits, glacé cherries, nuts and raisins – it looked really festive.

## Assorted Sweets

Your sweet-making talents may lie in the direction of nougat, coconut ice or Turkish Delight, all of which can be quite delicious if made at home. Fondant sweets come into this category; – standard fondant mixture can be coloured and flavoured to make a very attractive assortment. You can also make peppermint creams, sugar mice and other animal shapes. Children love shaped sweets and I know one confectioner who specialises in making a variety of really attractive animals based largely on the characters of Beatrix Potter. More modern characters could also be modelled in fondant.

## Truffles

Here again, the possibilities are enormous. Variations in flavour, coatings and texture can give you a unique collection of truffles. Popular flavours are rum, coffee and brandy but you could try more unusual ones such as orange liqueur, mixed nuts, cherry or pineapple – the last three can also help to vary the texture. Coatings can be chocolate powder, chocolate vermicelli, icing sugar and desiccated coconut as well as chocolate and white chocolate dips.

## Chocolates

Chocolate work is fairly specialised, but handmade chocolates can fetch a high price and if you do know a little bit about it, it could be well worth expanding your skills. All sorts of fillings can be used, but simple starters are fondant, truffle, marzipan and soft caramel.

Easter is a time when chocolate work comes into its own; some confectioners spend almost the whole period between Christmas and Easter making a store of Easter eggs and shapes. Rabbits and chickens are the traditional Easter shapes and you could extend the range to make all kinds of animals and round-the-year novelties. Dwarfs and cartoon characters are popular, but make sure that you are not infringing someone's franchise or copyright.

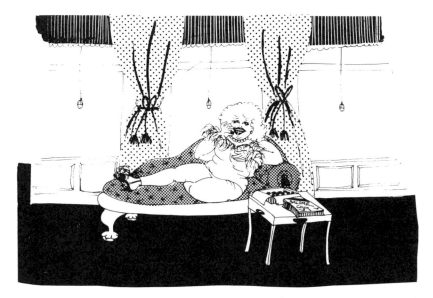

## Petit Fours

Petit fours fall into three main categories: marzipan-based sweets and shapes, small decorated almond biscuits and macaroons, and small assorted biscuits, decorated or chocolate-dipped. Sugar-dipped fruits are often included in a restaurant assortment but are not suitable for selling through any other type of outlet as they do not last for very long.

*Marzipan*

Marzipan is a sweetmeat which lends itself very well to modelling into shapes. Fruits, flowers and small animals made with carefully coloured marzipan can look surprisingly realistic.

*Crystallised Fruits*

Real crystallised fruits, if made and packed properly, will last for quite a long time. They are time-consuming to make as they must be worked on almost every day for a couple of weeks or more, but the actual processing is quite quick and easy after the initial preparation work. The care and attention required can be amply rewarded by the selling price, which is pretty high. Almost any kind of fruit can be crystallised successfully. Why not start with glacé pineapple rings, marrons glacé and sugar plums?

# PRESENTING YOUR PRODUCT

Many sweetmeats could be sold loose, and in certain instances this can work very well; some specialist chocolate shops or cake shops, for example, may not want to differentiate between their own lines and yours, or you may be selling to restaurants that will serve your produce on their own dishes.

However, the bulk of your sales is likely to be through luxury outlets, or outlets where an attractive package will immediately appeal to the eye and result in an impulse buy. Most of the sweetmeat ideas mentioned in this chapter could be bought as gifts, and packaging and presentation is naturally very important.

Decide at an early stage just what sort of packaging will be the best. There are two main considerations. You must show off the product to its best advantage, which usually means see-through material of some kind, and you must protect the product, which very often means the opposite! You will need to find a balance between the two requirements. Certainly, for small quantities of fudge or fondant creams, small Cellophane bags with metal twist ties will be quite sufficient. Chocolates and crystallised fruits may need more protection; chocolates show to good advantage in pleated paper cases, and crystallised fruits need to be packed in waxed paper. You will find that cardboard boxes with see-through polythene windows are best.

Labelling will be affected by the size and shape of the packaging. The 1980 Food Labelling Regulations exempt from some of the labelling requirements any prepacked food where the largest surface is less than ten square centimetres. Individually wrapped fancy confectionery products which are not enclosed in any further packaging and which are intended for sale as single items also carry an exemption.

You will need to study the various regulations fairly carefully. Sweets and chocolates, for example, are not classified as food for VAT purposes and this distinction carries through to other legislation – chocolate products are, in fact, covered by the Cocoa and Chocolate Products Regulations 1976 No 541 and The Cocoa and Chocolate Products (Amendment) Regulations 1982 No 17, rather than by the General Food Labelling Regulations.

## WHERE TO SELL

There are a number of different outlets that might be interested in selling your homemade sweetmeats.

### High Street Shops

Chocolate specialists are not usually interested in buying outside makes, but if you have something out of the ordinary to offer, such as chocolate models or a very special candy, they might be tempted to give it a go. A much better bet are confectionery shops and specialist patisseries. Very often these shops will also sell handmade chocolates, sweets and petit fours. High-class grocers with or without delicatessen counters may also be interested. All these outlets will probably be able to sell seasonal specialities as well as all-year lines.

### *Cafés, Teashops and Sandwich Bars*

The check-out counter at a café or teashop will often be stocked with mouthwatering items simply asking for an impulse buy. Homemade sweetmeats would fit in perfectly here. Sandwich bars may not immediately come to mind as good outlets, but I have known a sandwich bar catering for office workers specialise in Easter eggs and chocolate models and do a roaring trade during the run-up to Easter. In the Autumn they switched the emphasis to crystallised fruits and chocolates, with Christmas puddings as the winter speciality.

### *Craft Centres and Tourist Shops*

Fudge, toffee, coconut ice etc sell very well in tourist areas during the summer months, and if the sweetmeat has a local connection so much the better. Craft centres, too, are usually on the look out for further profit makers. Discuss your ideas with the proprietor first and choose items which fit in with the tone and atmosphere of the centre.

### *Restaurants and Hotels*

High labour costs, staff shortages and the advent of the freezer and the microwave now mean that few hotels employ more than one or two specialist chefs. There could be quite a market in this area for after-dinner specialities and petit fours.

## GETTING OFF THE GROUND

First of all, read and comply with the Food Hygiene (General) Regulations (see chapter 3). Then make a list of the specialist equipment that you will need, which will include some or all of the following items; depending on what you decide to make.

*Heavy aluminium pans.* Remember that as most types of candy will bubble up, you may need to increase the pan size by three or four times if you are doubling a recipe.

*Double pans,* for chocolate work

*Sugar thermometer.* Buy the best and the most accurate you can find because for many types of sweets the temperature is critical.

*Hydrometer,* for checking the density of sugar when making crystallised fruits

*Moulds,* for chocolates, fondants and models

*Trays and shallow tins,* for toffee, fudge and coconut ice

*Marble slab*, useful for chocolate, fondant and other fancy work

The next step is to put a price on your products and consider advertising and public relations. The action you take will depend upon the type of sweetmeats you are making and upon where and how you are selling them. A feature article in *Catering News,* for example, will be much more valuable to you if you are selling to restaurants and hotels then a local newspaper article, whereas local publicity will be just the thing for seasonal models, Easter eggs and Christmas candies.

# 9

# Celebration Cake Service

Successful cake-making and cake decorating require skill and experience. One cake decorator I know, who really does do the most beautiful cakes, started by going to evening classes. She had always enjoyed cooking but had never so much as decorated a Christmas cake before starting the course. Two years and many relatives' and friends' cakes later, she started to decorate cakes for people outside her immediate circle and is now in business full-time.

## CAKES FOR EVERY OCCASION

There are many, many occasions which can be celebrated with a special cake, and the scope for the cake decorator is enormous. There are birthdays, anniversaries, weddings, christenings, Easter and Christmas, to state the obvious ones. But have you thought of *every* possibility, and have you thought about how you might design the different cakes?

Start by making a list of all the times when people might like to have a specially decorated cake and put ideas for designs against

each one. This list will give you some valuable information. It will help you to decide whether to specialise in any particular area; it will help you to identify new business opportunities once you have your service established; and it will give you a handy reference for instant ideas to offer to a customer when discussing the design of a proposed cake.

## Cake-making Possibilities

*Birthdays*
These may be for any age from 1–100. Check the age being celebrated and, if the cake is for an adult, ask about hobbies and interests.

*Adult ideas*
Golf course, tennis court, barrel-organ with figures, crinoline lady, run-out pictures of hobby, cottages, castles etc.
*Children's ideas:* See below.

*Children's parties*
These may be for birthdays, Christmas or, indeed, held at any time of the year. Check hobbies.

*Ideas*
Wendy House, merry-go-round, run out of sports club badge, trains, engines and aeroplanes, cartoon characters.

*Bar mitzvah*
It is not part of the traditions of the bar mitzvah to have a cake, but if the celebration falls on the child's birthday then there will probably be one.

*Ideas*
Football, spaceships and satellites, musical instruments, vintage cars.

*Weddings*
How many tiers are required? Discuss the shape of the cake: round, square, cut-off corners or heart-shaped.

*Ideas*
Traditional decorations, perhaps with a touch of colour to match the flowers or the bridesmaids' dresses.

*Wedding anniversaries*
These could celebrate any anniversary from 1–50 or 60, but the later dates are ones which are usually celebrated. Check which anniversary it is, and check also on the couple's hobbies and interests.

*Ideas*
Replica of the house in which they live, local landmarks like Kent oasthouses or Suffolk windmills, or take your inspiration from the symbol of the anniversary.

*Wedding anniversary symbols*

| 1 Year | Paper | 20 Years | China | 35 Years | Coral | 50 Years | Gold |
|--------|-------|----------|-------|----------|-------|----------|------|
| 5 Years | Wood | 25 Years | Silver | 40 Years | Ruby | 55 Years | Emerald |
| 10 Years | Tin | 30 Years | Pearl | 45 Years | Sapphire | 60 Years | Diamond |
| 15 Years | Crystal | | | | | | |

*Christenings*
This is another traditional occasion. Many people like to use the symbolic blue for a boy and pink for a girl in the decoration, but a white cake with flowers and raised trellis work in the design usually proves the most popular.

*Celebration of success*
Some parties are held to celebrate success in a certain field, perhaps passing exams, winning a trophy, or promotion at work. Check on the reason for the celebration and take your inspiration from it.

*Ideas*
Swimming pool for a swimming trophy, a book or a run-out of the school badge for exams, and moneybags or a briefcase and rolled umbrella for promotion.

*Christmas cake*
These are traditionally round or square and decorated in white, but they do not have to be. Check ages of children in the family.

*Ideas*
Christmas crib, yule log, twelve days of Christmas, bells and Christmas trees.

*Other seasonal festivities*
These include Twelfth Night, St Valentine's Day, Mothering Sunday, Easter, Hallowe'en and Bonfire Night.

Twelfth Night cakes used to contain a special token and the person who received the piece of cake containing the token became the 'Lord' for the evening. Simnel Cakes, traditionally a Mothering Sunday speciality, are now often served at Easter; the twelve balls of marzipan round the top of the cake symbolise the twelve apostles. Other spring and Easter symbols are eggs, chicks and rabbits.

*Retirement parties*
Sometimes cakes are ordered to mark a retirement. This may take place at the business itself, or people may hold their own party at home. Check on the job and the interests and hobbies the person will now have to follow.

*Ideas:* Ledger with quill and ink, replica of place of work, wheelbarrow with flowers, artist's palette brushes, chessboard.

*Company or club anniversaries and jubilees*
Ideas for decoration are obviously going to be based upon the badge or insignia of the company or club or on its activities.

Most of the cake and design ideas I have given are based on the traditional fruit cake or on a sandwich or sponge cake base. Other countries use some different bases for their celebration cakes and it is perhaps worth adding one or two of these to your repertoire. In France or Italy, a cake made up of a pyramid of cream filled choux balls is often served at weddings; the French Christmas log has a chestnut and cream base; and other French and Austrian cakes have meringue or wafer-thin crispy sponge mixture bases. For ideas, have a look at a good book on foreign cakes or at *The Modern Patissier* by William Barker.

## STARTING UP

One of the advantages of cake decorating is that you need the minimum of equipment. A food mixer, some good mixing bowls and cake tins and a good selection of icing equipment is enough to get you started. You can then add to your stock of shaped tins and moulds as business builds. Buy flour, sugar and dried fruit in bulk and check whether you need any of the following:

Electric food mixer
Hand whip
Mixing bowls
Baking tray
Cake tins (variety of shapes)
Icing equipment, utensils and colours
Cake boards, stands and pillers
Non-edible decorations and ribbons
Stocks of edible decorations
Different sized cake boxes and collars

Think carefully about how you will package and deliver the cakes. You will need to protect them in transit with boxes and collars. Do remember to co-ordinate the sizes of your tins with the standard sizes of boxes and collars!

If you have a car, then delivery will present no problem. Evening deliveries are usually acceptable. If the venue is different from the client's address, try and deliver direct to be sure of an undamaged cake on the day.

## Pricing

The pricing of highly decorated cakes can be a difficult job. It is quite easy to work out the costs as outlined in chapter 4 but the main factor is time. One way to cost your time is to decide on an hourly rate and then to keep a record of how long every order takes to make. Remember to jot down the time spent at every stage. From these records you will be able to build up a range of charges for different kinds of work.

An alternative method of pricing is to check on the prices of similar cakes at a local cake shop or patissier and work from that, checking on actual costs each time.

# DESIGNING THE CAKES

The design of the cake is very important. There are plenty of pretty cakes around but a memorable cake needs to have that little bit extra. This will come from the imaginative use of colour in a wedding cake, an unusual or highly appropriate shape for a celebratory cake, or the clever use of special icing techniques for anniversary and other cakes. Sometimes all the different techniques are used together to get the required effect. Run-out pictures for example, can be over-piped round the edge to define detail.

Wherever possible, get together with your client and discuss the cake in detail. The following check list gives the points you should cover.

*Check List for Discussion with the Customer*
1. What is the cake for? The occasion itself could suggest a design.
2. Does the customer have any particular design ideas? If the answer is yes, you can save a lot of time by going straight into a discussion on how it might be achieved.
3. In the case of a wedding, has the customer considered the use of colour? If a colour is agreed, ask for a piece of material from a bridesmaid's dress or other appropriate reference. This is important because the words pink or blue could mean very many different shades.
4. If they might want to keep the top tier of the wedding cake for a possible Christening, you should warn them that after a while the oil from the marzipan will start to discolour the icing and the cake may need to be re-iced.
5. For anniversaries, birthdays and celebrations, find out about hobbies and interests. These could lead to ideas for design.
6. Show photographs of other cakes you have made to spark off an idea for which you already have design notes and templates.
7. How far does the cake have to be transported and does it have to be moved again once it has been delivered? The answers to these questions could prohibit the use of lace collars, for exam-

ple, which are very fragile indeed. One cake decorator I know insists on her husband driving her on deliveries while she sits on the back seat tenderly nursing the cake!

8. How much is the customer prepared to pay? The execution of the design idea will depend a great deal on the answer. Do not get too carried away early on in the discussions. Frills and edgings need to have replacements made in case of accidental damage to the cake, and a good plaque can take almost as long to make as the cake itself. The phrase 'time is money', is particularly true of cake decorating.

Some experienced cake decorators avoid run-out pictures because they say that they cannot draw. But drawing is not really necessary; all you need to be able to do is to trace from somebody else's picture. Use a simple Christmas card design for Christmas cakes, a magazine drawing or advertisement for sports or hobbies or pictures in books for specialist activities. Make templates by tracing over the pictures and do remember to keep them for future use – you may even be able to sell the same idea to your next customer!

Do not be afraid of using humour. One of the funniest cakes, and for that reason one of the most memorable and talked about, that I have ever come across played on the fact that the boy whose birthday it was hated brushing his teeth and was not too keen on bathing either. The cake was made in the shape of a bath and on top it were various items, including a toothbrush and a set of false teeth! Warning: do make sure that the recipient also has a sense of humour!

The design of the cake must start with the shape, as this will affect the proportions of the plaques or the placing of sprays and figures. For some designs the cake may need to be deeper or shallower than usual. Wedgwood-type plaques, for example, need a deep-sided cake, whereas a chessboard looks a little odd if the cake is very deep. A flat-sided cake is also much easier for plaques as round ones mean that the plaques, too, must be curved.

Next, work out in detail all the work that will be required. Set out the list in time order, and decide on the type of cake base required. This will probably be determined by the type of icing you are planning to use. Butter, water and fondant icings are fine on sponge and sandwich bases, but a fruit cake base will be needed for the heavier icings and for marzipan.

# MAKING THE CAKE

Everyone who is thinking about cake decoration as a money-making activity will have their own recipes and be experienced in the techniques required. However, it is always useful to hear what other experts have to say. So here is a round-up of helpful hints and tips on how to avoid the common disasters – and how to put them right or camouflage them if they happen.

*The Fruit*
Most recipes say 'clean or pick over' the fruit; the experts recommend that the fruit is washed very well and then dried thoroughly.

If brandy or any other alcohol is being used in the cake, soak the fruit in it. This gives a much nicer taste. However it also uses more alcohol and should be costed accordingly. When you come to put the fruit in the cake, dry it again and sprinkle with flour taken from that weighed out for the cake – *not* an extra amount.

*Lining the Cake*
Whatever the size and shape of the cake, line the inside of the tin with greaseproof or parchment paper and the outside with brown paper. Most cakes will need two or three layers of brown paper, and extra large cakes will need four layers of brown paper and two layers of greaseproof or parchment paper.

If the sides of the cake do catch and burn a little, grate off the offending part with a fine grater. Never try to cut it off with a knife.

*The Top of the Cake*
If the top of the cake gets a little too hard and crusty, start by rub-

bing it with a fine grater, but do not carry the operation too far or you will catch the fruit. Brush with equal parts of glycerine and sherry to soften up the surface before putting the marzipan in place.

The surface for decorating must be really flat. A slightly risen cake can be built up with marzipan, but if the dome is too high it should be cut off and the cake turned over so that the base is used as the decorating surface. Use a spirit level to check that the top is completely flat all over.

### Icing Equipment

It is extremely important to ensure that no fat or grease gets near to any of the icing equipment or it will spoil the icing. Items such as spoons, cups or basins which are used for icing should be kept solely for that purpose. Start by scalding them and then scouring with salt. Scald them again and they are then ready for use.

### Colours for Icing

There are plenty of proprietary icing colours on the market, but strong colours can sometimes present something of a problem. Try using powdered rather than liquid colours and experiment with the edible dyes used in Indian cooking. Most Indian grocers sell these.

### Protecting the Icing

Icing usually needs to be kept covered with a damp cloth in order to keep it workable. Use a piece of old sheeting or muslin which has been washed many times. If the tiniest piece of fluff gets into the icing it could block up the smallest piping and writing tubes.

### Protecting Roses and Other Decorations

Place made-up roses in tissue-lined egg boxes for protection.

### Icing Disasters

A slightly bubbly icing surface can be corrected by rubbing lightly with very fine sandpaper. This only works on white icing; with coloured icing the sandpaper breaks through to the white sugar crystals to give a speckled effect.

Icing which cracks across the top can be flooded out and redried, but if you do not have time to do this the crack can be covered with decorations. Side and corner imperfections can be covered with ribbon or with star tube piping.

The worst disaster I came across involved a lady who accidently leant with her elbow on the top of a newly decorated cake. She did not have time to flood out the top again and so she camouflaged the depression with a beautiful basket of roses!

Another disaster I heard about happened because the cake decorator decided to dry out her plaques in the airing cupboard. A few hours later, a member of her family put a very damp bath towel in the cupboard and the plaques disintegrated.

## GETTING YOUR NAME KNOWN

Local advertising in the weekly newspaper can be useful for wedding cakes, as can direct mail. Many cake decorators advertise on shop notice boards. A more sophisticated form of advertising is to link up with a cake shop that does not specialise in cakes to order. Read the sections on advertising and promotion in chapter 4.

It is a good idea to write to all the catering firms in your area telling them about your services and enclosing a small stock of cards and leaflets. Very often customers will ask their caterer to recommend someone to make the cake.

In running a cake decorating business, as in any other kind of business, quality and service are very important. A series of memorable cakes will soon get you talked about and this form of advertising is as useful as any. A consistently high standard will also give you the edge over competitors who may be cutting corners.

If your business is large enough, you might also consider having your business name and an advertising slogan printed on your cake boxes. Other ideas worth thinking about include offering a small extra service, such as the loan of a pretty cake knife or a large sharp knife for a large cake. You could always include a short wedding check list on your promotional literature, perhaps a reminder of things often forgotten or a guide to wedding etiquette.

# 10

# Wine Bar Food and Pub Grub

Selling to other catering outfits can be a sort of home catering half-way house; you can take on as much or as little work as you think that you can cope with, and you can combine it with other activities such as cooking for dinner parties, making country foods or running a packed lunch or picnic service. However, you must be prepared to produce and deliver on a regular basis – if you have agreed to supply so many pies or pounds of pâté every Monday you cannot one week just decide that you do not feel up to it. If you do not deliver regularly, you will soon lose all your business.

## FINDING YOUR OUTLETS

Some areas are full of pubs, many of which offer bar snacks or have restaurants. In town centres and also in suburban areas, wine bars have sprung up offering a variety of meals and snacks. Take a look in your local Yellow Pages to see how many such establishments are listed and where they are located. You could try driving or walking round your immediate neighbourhood to see what possible outlets there are.

If you have time, go into the wine bars or pubs and check the food already on sale. Make notes on the location and menu of each establishment. Look for gaps in the repertoire and for ideas which could help extend the business. When you get home, sort out your list into those places which you think will be worth approaching and those which are either well catered for already or which do not place any emphasis on food at all.

*'I know it's a posh restaurant, Harold, but do we have to dress up?'*

Keep your ear to the ground while you are doing your research and maybe you will hear of a new place about to open. Obviously, if you can get in at the start it will be to your advantage.

Your final list of potential outlets should include some or all of the following types of catering establishments.

### Wine Bars

Most wine bars will be selling food already. But it could be that there are gaps in what is offered which you might be able to fill, or you might be able to think of a different way of doing things which would help the manager (or owner) to compete with a nearby establishment. Suggest ideas for food which would be particularly complementary to special wines: a course country pâté with a French red wine, homemade sausages and sliced cold meats with German wine and pasta with Italian wine. You never know, you might find customers among those who are otherwise well served.

### Pubs and Inns

Pubs tend to sell more traditional and less sophisticated food than wine bars but there is still scope for new ideas. Homemade bread, raised pies, and homemade sausages are the sorts of food that might go well here. Desserts or sweet snacks are also worth thinking about. They are not often served in pubs but lots of people like to indulge a sweet tooth. When assessing the food on sale, look at the area the pub serves and think about the tastes of the clientele.

### Restaurants and Hotels

Quite a few restaurants and hotels are cutting down on the number of chefs they employ and are using either ready-prepared frozen produce or are offering a range of less elaborate dishes than they used to. This means that the manager may be interested in buying in specialist items such as homemade bread, petit fours, raised pies, and gâteaux. Talk to the owner or manager and see if there are any gaps in the menu that you could fill.

### Snack and Sandwich Bars

These are essentially a town centre or city phenomenon and they are, of course, mainly concerned with selling sandwiches. However, some of them do offer quiches and a variety of individual pies, so if there are some sandwich bars within easy reach do explore the possibility of extending their range.

### Cafés and Teashops

As well as specialising in cakes and scones, some of these establishments also offer a light luncheon and snack menu. This is where your produce could find another outlet. Likely items are quiches, pasties and pâtés.

# WHAT TO MAKE

The choice of what you make will depend upon your assessment of outlets, upon your discussions with the owners or managers, and also upon your own skills and inclinations.

*'He should never have had that second helping of sherry trifle.'*

### Pâtés, Terrines, Pies and Sausages

All these items are covered in some detail in chapter 7, Country Foods. Choose recipes that will suit the particular type of establishment you have in mind and the kind of food and drink that it sells. Traditional dishes or recipes with an old-fashioned flavour are becoming increasingly popular.

Homemade pastry dishes always go well. These include Bacon and Egg Pies, Pork Pies, Steak and Kidney Pies, Custard Tarts, Apple Tarts, etc.

One pub I came across specialises in individual baked pies with a top crust only. A local cook makes the pies in small earthenware pots and they are covered in uncooked pastry before delivery. The pies are then cooked in the pub kitchen's large commercial oven. Fillings include beef with beer and prunes, veal, ham and egg, chicken, bacon and mushroom, lamb and stout, and the ever-popular steak and kidney.

### Quiches and Flans

Quiches and flans are very popular. Quiches can be filled with a variety of different ingredients: bacon, sweetcorn and chopped sausages go down well in down-to-earth areas, whereas blue cheese, smoked fish or courgettes may be appreciated in more sophisticated places. You may even consider making a sweet quiche with cottage cheese and dates or apricots.

A plain scrambled egg flan decorated with sliced tomatoes and cooked peas can be a best-seller in a local wine bar, and a cold chicken flan set with aspic in a city sandwich bar. Sweet flans sell well almost everywhere.

### Soups, Stews and Casseroles

Many outlets which specialise in cold food like to offer either soup or one hot dish-of-the-day but do not make their own. If you can come up with reasonably competitive prices, your homemade foods should prove much more popular than bought-in commercially frozen foods or catering packs of dried or canned soup. Stick to fairly simple beef, pork or chicken casseroles and be more adventurous with your soups.

### Salads

This is another area where the home caterer may be able to plug a gap in a commercial caterer's organisation. Cheese pies and pâtés can all be bought from large manufacturers, but most salads need to be made on the same day as they are to be eaten.

It is fairly difficult to predict what salads customers will like, so once you have agreed an outline policy with the manager, make small quantities of the more unusual salads and see how they go. Step up the amounts if you find they are running out very quickly.

*Desserts*

Instead of competing with the large manufacturers who make Black Forest Gateaux and cheesecakes why not have your own specialities. Home made meringues or Meringue Gateaux, for example, are much nicer than the 'plaster of Paris' versions sold commercially. Or you might try your hand at making a choux or flaky pastry gateaux, or regional or traditional desserts. Do some research and see if you cannot come up with a local recipe for Tipsy Pudding or Syllabub.

# GETTING OFF THE GROUND

You must first organise your activities on a commercial basis: study the Food Hygiene Regulations and the other legislation set out in chapter 3, and decide upon accountancy procedures and pricing policy.

## Making the Approach

To find your outlets, look at your list of possibles and then go and have a few meals at the most likely places to see what the management is trying to achieve. When you come to talk to the proprietor or manager he will have much more time for you if you can show that you understand his business.

*Points for Discussion*
1. Give details of the gap in their service which you think needs to

be filled, or the way in which you think that they can increase business or compete more successfully.
2. Show how your products could fill the gap or achieve an increase in business.
3. Explain your qualifications for offering such a service, perhaps by taking along some samples of your cooking.
4. Give your prices and proposed delivery structure.

You will need to be both tactful and flexible. No one wants to be told that their operation is poor – particularly by someone who does not have much experience in the field! Happily most people are open to new suggestions.

## Making and Preserving the Food

Food for these outlets must be as fresh as possible; for some items you might need to look into the question of preservatives. Pubs and wine bars often have pies, pâtés and terrines on show and they are not always in a chiller cabinet. If the whole quantity is not eaten, it may then be returned to the fridge and brought out again the next day.

There are very strict rules concerning the use of preservatives in food for sale and these are covered by the Preservatives in Food Regulations (1979) No 752 and the Preservatives in Food (Amendment) Regulations (1982) No 15. These regulations list permitted preservatives and specify foods in which they may be used.

Provided that you make the food immediately prior to delivery and you do not deliver more than a reasonable amount at any one time, you will probably be better off not using any additives. Your homemade reputation will therefore not suffer and your products will have the good homemade flavour that sells. In this case, you should make sure that those in charge of the food know that it does not contain any preservatives and that it should be kept chilled whenever possible.

You can enhance the flavour, and to some extent the keeping properties, of items like pâtés and terrines by using alcohol in the recipe or by making sure that it is well sealed with a thick layer of butter or aspic. *Never freeze any food which is going to another catering establishment* as there is a risk of double freezing and consequent contamination.

## Presenting the Food

Even the tastiest food can look uninteresting unless it is well presented and foil containers sitting on the bar or counter do not really inspire confidence. If you are delivering to an outlet on a regular basis, it would be quite easy to pick up the empty used containers from the previous delivery. You might think about using special earthenware containers, perhaps colour coded to contents, and investing in some attractive labels.

Any facts about the food which you can give the landlord, wine bar manager or restaurant owner could be used to attract customers. Information on traditional recipes or foods using local ingredients can be chalked up on the daily food board in the bar, typed on labels for the buffet or included on a handwritten or printed menu.

These selling tips will only enhance a good product; they will not shift a mediocre one. As with all areas of cooking from home, a consistently high standard is your best guarantee of success.

# 11

# Running a Freezer Service

This is potentially the most capital intensive of all the money-making activities covered in this book. Freezers are expensive to buy, the packaging requirements are high and some businesses have felt the need to move into special premises fairly early on in their operation.

It is possible to combine a limited freezer service with one or two other activities and, indeed, some of the freezer service cooks I talked to had started out in other areas and had developed their freezer sections in response to demand from their existing clients.

Jean Pierre of Jean Pierre's Pantry, for example, started off cooking for high-class dinner parties. Then some of his clients asked if he could provide food for weekend house parties or help to cater for visitors. The obvious answer was to provide frozen food. A similar story is told by Jenny Raglan of Raglan Catering Services: some of her clients wanted to have a stock of food for short-notice business entertaining, and frozen food was the answer.

Once your frozen food service has got going, it can bring in business for your other catering activities. A customer who likes your frozen items may decide to try your services for a special party or a wedding breakfast.

# WHAT SORT OF SERVICE?

There are three distinct types of frozen food service. The choice will depend on what else you are doing and how you see your business developing. You could combine all three or mix one of them with another home-cooking activity.

## *Selection of Dishes*

Making a selection of one-off single- or family-portion dishes for the customer to choose from has a number of advantages. You can use slack days to add to the stocks in your freezer, batch-cooking one dish at a time. Unless the order is a large one, the customer will come to you to collect the food, and there is also potential for growth by selling through other retail outlets.

The problem of success is that you can quickly run out of freezer space and you may have to consider finding larger premises for batch cooking and storage, perhaps with a shop front for extra sales. Jean Pierre's Pantry, for example, operates from a very well-equipped shop in Battersea, London. The company was lucky to find premises which had been equipped by another catering company, otherwise the costs would have been very high.

### Complete Meals

Complete meals can be made up from one-portion dishes offered on a selection service list, but this is a waste of packaging if a large party is to be catered for. Very often hostesses like to pass off a catered meal as their own work and this is quite easy if they buy a ready-frozen meal!

The service is usually a very personal one, the menu being discussed with each client individually. It ties in well with a dinner party or large-scale catering service. Popular dishes from your menus can be made ahead so that slack time can be put to good use.

### Filling Service

Some people like to have their freezer filled for them. This saves them the bother of sorting out the mysteries of bulk buying or having to cook for the freezer. Both new and existing freezer owners are potential customers, and if you have enough clients such a service could keep you very busy.

## GETTING STARTED

In addition to the general considerations outlined in chapter 2, you will need to assess the volume of business you are likely to handle and to decide how much space you will need for preparation and storage.

Do some basic market research on your area and see if there are any shops that might be interested in stocking your frozen foods. If the results are favourable you should consider setting up a limited company, as this is the sort of business that will benefit from such a set up. Remember, too, that loans are available to small businesses through various government schemes, and you could discuss this with your bank manager.

Initial costs are going to include items under the following headings:

> Modifications to either your own kitchen or new premises outside your home
> New freezers
> Bulk preparation equipment
> Bulk buying of packaging materials
> Bulk printing of labels
> Ingredients for initial stocks

Insurance is very important if you run a freezer business. In addition to the points raised on the subject in chapter 2, the contents of each freezer will need to be insured. Consult an insurance broker about the best policies to take out.

Both the Food Hygiene (General) Regulations and the Food Labelling Regulations are relevant in the sale of frozen foods. Read the sections covering these regulations in chapter 3, and look at the specimen label on page 136.

# WHAT TO MAKE

What you make will vary according to the type of service you are planning to offer.

## Selection of Single-portion Dishes

The first point to make about selecting dishes for a frozen food list is *do not try and include too many*. Twelve to 16 dishes will give you a good enough range and you will be able to standardise your recipes and methods of preparation. Choice of dishes will depend upon the answers to the following questions:

## *What dishes are always popular?*

First, look at the range of speciality frozen foods offered by other small producers. Look also at the menus of reasonably priced restaurants and, if you have done any kind of catering before, draw on your own experience. Dishes like Beef Bourguignon, Coq au Vin and Duck à l'orange are bound to figure high on all these lists. Whether or not you decide to compete with these particular dishes, they do give you a lead as to what people like to have when they are not cooking themselves. Look for other dishes which take time to prepare and cook something which might appeal in the same way.

Stews or casseroles are popular for informal entertaining, with single people and with couples who cannot be bothered to go to the trouble of cooking for the two of them. But one word of warning: most people are fairly conservative so do not be too way-out in your selection. A familiar item or two on the list is always reassuring to the potential buyer.

It is also a good idea to include one or two more economical dishes in your range to attract those who want a quick meal with no effort and not too much cost.

## *What dishes freeze well?*

This is important. You will gain customers by the quality of your food, and it is vital to choose dishes which will show no signs of having been frozen. Most stews and casseroles fall into this category, but take care with highly spiced dishes as the flavour can intensify or even alter slightly in the freezer. Vanilla and nutmeg are particularly prone to change when frozen.

Pastry dishes freeze well, but if the dish is for sale, it is advisable to freeze the dish before the pastry is cooked, not afterwards. This way, you will avoid any problems which might arise on thawing, such as a soggy pastry base.

Soups, pâtés, mousses, gateaux and baked pasta dishes also freeze well. The latter, like pastry dishes, are best frozen before the final baking.

Avoid dishes containing hard-boiled eggs as the whites go very rubbery, and remember that sauces tend to thicken a little on freezing.

Most of the dishes mentioned above are easy to batch cook, and this is a very important consideration when cooking for a frozen food service.

## What dishes are you good at making?

If you hate making pastry, for example, there is no point in specialising in pies and tarts. You will be making quite a lot of your chosen items and it makes sense to choose those which you can cook with enjoyment and confidence.

After considering all these points a sample list may look something like this:

*Starters/entrées*
Vichyssoise
Shrimp Bisque
Chicken Liver and Bacon Pâté
Smoked Haddock Mousse

*Main courses*
Beef Bourguignon
Beef and Guinness Pie
Veal Marengo
Lamb and Orange Casserole
Coq au Vin
Somerset Cidered Chicken
New England Fish Pie
Moussaka
Lasagne

*Desserts*
Lemon Mousse
Fruit Sorbet
Spiced Apple Pie

The next step is to adapt your recipes for larger-scale catering and try them out. You will need to know exactly how many portions of a standard weight a given amount will yield – and you need to be pretty sure that the recipe will always work out this way as you must give the weight of the dish on the label. You also need to be sure that the dish will freeze well and you must work out thawing instructions which are simple to follow and foolproof.

With the growing interest in healthy eating, you might like to think about specialising in frozen dishes made from wholefoods. Vegetarian dishes are a logical extension, and the Pine Nut Pantry in Kent specialises in a range of vegetarian food which includes dishes like Vegetable Lasagne, Spaghetti and Bean Bake, Red Chilli Bean Pancakes and Date and Apple Crumble.

## Menu Selection for Complete Meals

Considerations similar to those for the selection of individual dishes also apply here, but the scope can be a little wider. Have a look at the menu planning sections in chapter 13, Cooking for Dinner Parties, and in chapter 14, Catering in Quantity, and then apply the criterion of whether the dishes will freeze well.

Err on the side of over-caution: there is nothing worse that being served a soggy-based quiche or cheesecake when you know how good the freshly-cooked equivalent can be.

You will need to consider how the dish is to be served. It is no good offering a traditional Steak and Kidney Pie if it has to be cooked and presented on an elegant buffet table in a large foil container.

Here is a selection of items which appeared on my London Cooks frozen food lists. Dishes were available for two or more.

*Starters*
   Smoked Trout Mousse with Tomato Sauce
   Normandy Liver Terrine
   Avocado Bisque

Minestrone
Smoked Beef and Ham Pâté
Chilled Ratatouille
Barbecued Spare Ribs

*Main Courses*
Baked Mackerel with Gooseberry Sauce
Chicken in Cider Cream Sauce
Chicken Marengo
Beef à la mode
Duck à l'orange
Spiced Pork with Orange
Beef Provençal
Chicken with Peaches
Super-Fish Pie
Chilli Con Carne

*Vegetables*
Braised Chicory
Celery and Cabbage Casserole
Courgettes à la Provençale
Broad Beans in Parsley Sauce
Purée of Jerusalem Artichokes and Potatoes
Baked Red Cabbage

*Desserts*
Brandy Raisin Ice Cream Gâteau
French Lemon Tart
Gooseberry Pie
Pears in Red Wine
Chocolate Orange Mousse
Apricot Gâteau
Cassata

All these items were chosen on the basis of their popularity in general catering and their suitability for freezing. As each item was ordered for the first time, thawing and finishing-off instructions were prepared and duplicated so that sets would be available for use with future orders.

## Food for a Filling Service

A filling service can only be offered on a very individual basis. Guidelines can be given on the percentage allocation of space in the freezer for different categories of food, but the final decision must depend on the life style and the requirements of the freezer owner.

Much of the saving gained from having a freezer lies in the ability to store food which has been bought in bulk. This is fine if the client has a large family, but half a cow for two people could mean that they will get very bored with beef! It may also be that the client does not want to do very much cooking and is interested in the freezer as a source of instant meals.

So go along to see your clients with an open mind. Talk to them to see how they view the use of their freezer and how they see it helping to enhance their life style. This sort of conversation will help you to get the right balance. But beware of too great an enthusiasm in one area – remember that there may be other members of the family who are not present at the discussion – and make sure that the meat-lovers, for example, have some ready-cooked dishes as well as steaks, chops and joints, which all take time to thaw out.

### Allocation of Freezer Space

This general guide to the allocation of freezer space can easily be adopted to suit individual requirements.

20% Home- and commercially-frozen meat, fish and poultry
20% Home- or commercially-frozen fruit and vegetables
30% Home-cooked and frozen produce for everyday needs
10% Home-cooked and frozen produce for entertaining
10% Commercially-frozen convenience foods
 5% Stand-by ingredients
 5% Spare capacity

Home-cooked and frozen produce for everyday meals might include a selection of soups and starters, casseroles, baked pasta, rice and potato dishes sweet and savoury pies desserts and bread and cakes. Discuss this section in some detail with your clients. Freeze some items in family quantities and some in individual packs to give maximum flexibility.

Food for entertaining should follow the guidelines given earlier in the chapter. Make sure that your instructions include notes on presentation.

Stand-by items are part of the convenience aspects of a freezer, and if your customer does any cooking at all he or she will find them extremely useful. Suggested items include breadcrumbs, grated cheese, ready-made pastry and crumble toppings, stock, basic sauces and fruit purées.

Spare capacity is useful to allow for advance preparation for a major party or to freeze items from the garden during the summer months.

Bulk-buying for the remaining 40% capacity can be quite a tricky operation and you must be sure of your suppliers. This is particularly important for meat, which must be of the highest quality and hung for the correct period of time. If you are planning to freeze all the produce in your own freezer, make sure that you have a good freezer book which covers the basic principles of freezing and gives step by step instructions for each type of produce. If you are not sure how to freeze correctly, ask the butcher to freeze the meat for you and buy in commercially frozen fish, fruit and vegetables.

# PACKING IT AWAY

## The Freezer

There are two types of freezer to choose from: the chest freezer and the upright freezer. Very often the choice is a matter of space. Whichever type you choose it is important to be sure that it is capable of operating continuously at 0°F/−18°C.

There should not be any appreciable increase in the temperature of food already stored when fresh food is being frozen, and to be sure of this choose a freezer which has a fast-freezing section or compartment. Take care never to overload this section of the freezer. A speedier preparation is simply not worth the risk of damaging the rest of your stock.

A chest freezer with a simple opening lid is ideal for bulk storage of food and should be used if you can possibly find the space. There is very little loss of cold air when the lid is opened because cold air is heavier than warm air and stays in the freezer. This is important both in keeping down the running costs and in keeping a constant temperature in the freezer. In contrast, the upright freezer loses its cold air every time it is opened and this can cause temperature fluctuations in the cabinet. Electricity consumption will be higher and the freezer will need to be defrosted more often.

The disadvantage of a chest freezer is that the different dishes can get mixed up. However, divider baskets easily solve this problem. Make sure you make a basket for each product line.

## Packaging Material

Packaging materials must be robust and able to stand up to the wear and tear of freezer storage. They must also be suitable for the job in hand. Heavy-duty polythene bags, for example, are fine for home use but foil containers are very much better for retail use.

Use small foil containers for single portions and very large ones for party catering. The advantage of foil containers is that customers can pop them straight into the oven to re-heat or to cook. The food can then be transferred to a dinner plate or a large casserole or dish for serving. Foil containers also have matching lids, to which can be attached the necessary labels giving details of weight, contents and maker.

If you are running a freezer filling service, you will need to invest in heavy-duty aluminium foil and polythene bags. These can be bought in bulk from your cash-and-carry or from suppliers like Lakeland Plastics.

## Labelling

The sample label shown below illustrates very clearly all the points covered in the Food Labelling Regulations for frozen food. This is a printed label but the information given applies equally to hand-written labels.

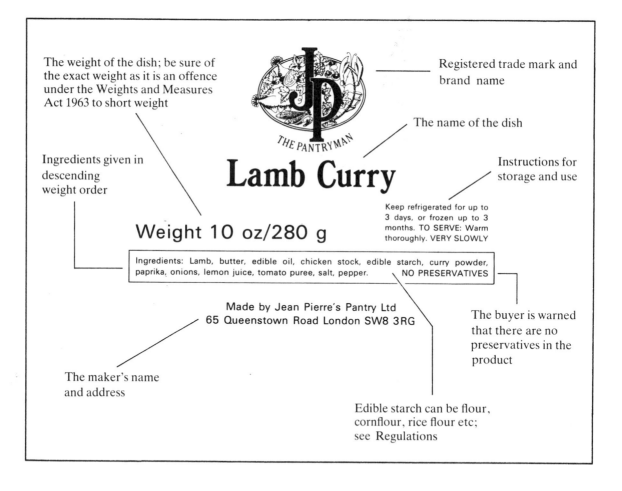

The weight of the dish; be sure of the exact weight as it is an offence under the Weights and Measures Act 1963 to short weight

Ingredients given in descending weight order

Registered trade mark and brand name

The name of the dish

Instructions for storage and use

THE PANTRYMAN

**Lamb Curry**

Keep refrigerated for up to 3 days, or frozen up to 3 months. TO SERVE: Warm thoroughly. VERY SLOWLY

Weight 10 oz/280 g

Ingredients: Lamb, butter, edible oil, chicken stock, edible starch, curry powder, paprika, onions, lemon juice, tomato puree, salt, pepper.    NO PRESERVATIVES

Made by Jean Pierre's Pantry Ltd
65 Queenstown Road London SW8 3RG

The buyer is warned that there are no preservatives in the product

The maker's name and address

Edible starch can be flour, cornflour, rice flour etc; see Regulations

# GETTING YOUR NAME KNOWN

In the early days of running a freezer service your stocks are likely to be limited and local publicity will be your main objective. Read the relevant sections in chapter 4 to see which methods of advertising and promotion are likely to suit your area the best.

A leaflet giving details of your service, lists of available dishes and, if you are difficult to find, a map showing where the food can be picked up, is very useful. It can be used for direct mail shots and as back-up to accompany personal letters and press releases.

Once you get going you may like to consider other ideas for helping people to remember your name and your service. One such idea is to print a useful list of freezer tips on one side of a sheet of paper, with the thawing and finishing instructions of your dish on the other. Alternatively, include the hints on your instruction leaflet. You could offer to write a short piece on freezer management for the local paper or county magazine, or to speak on the subject on local radio. Make sure that you make a reference to bought-in goods and your own range of products and ask for a by-line or for the programme presenter or introduction to say 'Katy Smith of Katy's Kitchen'. As the business grows, you could try and interest a national magazine in your activities to see if you could get your name known to a wider audience.

# 12
# Lunch Boxes and Picnics

Depending upon the area in which you live, a lunch box and picnic service could be built into a profitable business. Alternatively, it could be combined with a dinner party or freezer service.

If you do not want to do too much work at first, this sort of service will be a good way to start catering from home as you will not need to invest much money in new equipment or in packaging. Provided that you have a well equipped kitchen, you could probably get away with an initial purchase of plastic cutlery and cups, paper plates and boxes. Anything more elaborate could be hired as and when needed.

However, if you are planning a fairly large business you will need, first of all, to check the Food Hygiene (General) Regulations and to talk to your local health inspector. Follow this up with some market research, and then decide what sort of lunch box or picnic package would be the most successful.

## WHO WILL BUY?

Read the section on market research in chapter 4 and try to assess your area in the same way. Make a list of the possible sources of business and note the type of work that they might generate.

*Business Sources and Possible Requirements*

*Business offices*
Individual desk-top lunches for executives on their own or for small meetings.

*Businesses and associations*
Coach party outings for the staff, VIP trips to special events, PR visits to sporting events, etc.

*Private individuals*
Picnic parties to outdoor events such as horse shows, county shows, race meetings and other sporting events.

*Families*
Children's party boxes for both indoor and outdoor parties and for picnics.

Check on the shows and events in your area during the year and make a note of the dates for future reference for advertising and promotion.

# THE BOX AND ITS CONTENTS

What sort of boxes are you going to use and what sort of food are you going to put in them? The answers to these questions will, of course, be dictated largely by the type of event you are catering for and the price that the client is prepared to pay. But they will also be affected by such considerations as the time of year, ease of packing and susceptibility to damage. The food must also be chosen for ease of eating outdoors with fork or fingers.

Presentation is equally important. A large whole raised pie will look extremely appetising as part of a hamper full of food, but it may not look so good when it has been cut up into pieces for individual picnic boxes; small pies will look a lot better. Indeed, anything which can be made and cooked in single portions will look much more attractive in individual picnic boxes. Conversely, whole roast chickens, large quiches and pies, and set moulds of jellies look marvellous in a hamper for six, eight or ten.

Don't avoid offering delicate items like mousses, pâtés and jellied salads and desserts such as trifles, cream puddings and whips. They can easily be made and packed in small tubs. But do remember to label them. A trifle for starter and a chicken liver pâté for dessert can be rather off-putting!

Your ideas will need to be fairly flexible as the requirements for each event can be very different. Nevertheless, it is sensible to have some ideas at the ready so that you can make suggestions if potential clients do not know exactly what they want.

Have a look at these suggestions and at those included in the cold finger and fork buffet menus listed in chapter 14, Catering In Quantity. Remember that you will have to pack food into a picnic box and this in itself will eliminate some items.

*Desk-top lunches*

Scotch Eggs
Stuffed Ham Rolls
Smoked Haddock Quiche
Brown Bread Rolls and Butter
Custard Tart

Individual Pork Pies
Stuffed Crispy Rolls
Asparagus Quiche
Cheese and Biscuits

Pâté de Campagne
Chicken and Mushroom Pie
Stilton and Cheddar Cheese
French bread and Butter
Apples and Grapes

Cheesy Sausage Rolls
Open Barncakes or Open Sandwiches
Mushroom and Bacon Flan
Mixed Fruit Bowl

*Conference baskets*

Coated Chicken Drumsticks with Crisps
Stuffed Tomatoes with Lettuce
Individual Ham Quiches
French Bread and Butter
Apricot Mousse
Cheese and Biscuits

Cornish Pasties with Crisps
Stuffed Eggs
Cold Spiced Sausages with Tomatoes
Crispy Buttered Rolls
Apple Pie

### Special event picnic boxes

Chicken and Ham Pie
Roast Beef Rolls with Potato Salad
Mixed Green Salad and Tomatoes
Crispy Rolls with Butter
Individual Trifles
Brie and Biscuits

Salmon Mousse
Roast Turkey and Ham Slices with Trimmings
Mushrooms à la Grecque
Bean and Corn Salad
Tomato and Chicory
Brown Rolls and Butter
Chocolate Mousse
French Cheese and Biscuits

### Picnic hampers

Taramasalata
Hummous
Cold Spiced Roast Chicken
Ham in Parsley Aspic
Coleslaw
Potato and Tomato Salads
Crusty Farmhouse Bread and Butter
Camembert and Biscuits
Fruit

Smoked Trout Pâté with Brown Bread and Butter
Cold Roast Breast of Duck with Orange Salad
Cold Lamb Cutlets in Aspic
Savoury Rice Salad
Tomato and Avocado Salad
Homemade Bread Rolls and Butter

Stilton and Smoked Ilchester Cheese
Strawberries and Cream

Cold-weather picnics and hampers could also include thermos flasks of hot soup.

Cardboard cake boxes in various sizes should be sufficient for packing most lunches and picnics but wicker baskets may be required for special occasions. Presentation is always important, and once you get established it might be worth having small cloth-covered baskets for conference table lunches, coloured or patterned cake boxes for desk-top lunches or children's parties, and hampers for race meetings or horse shows.

### Children's Parties

Children's party boxes are rather different to adults' picnic boxes in that children are not very interested in sophisticated food. They tend to go for the old favourites like sausages and sausage rolls, cornish pasties, quiches and good old-fashioned sandwiches. This means that presentation is very important. Anything which is fun to look at, to eat out of or to play with will go down well – and remember that a child's sense of humour is rather basic.

Put funny faces on the tops of pies and rolls, make interestingly shaped food and use bright colours. Remember to include some crisps and sweets as well as the proper food, and stick mainly to savoury items. It is also quite a good idea to include novelties or wrapped surprises in the boxes, and if there is any kind of a theme to the party then tie in the colours, shapes and novelties with the theme.

## Pricing the Boxes

Pricing is fairly straightforward as there are not too many hidden overheads. Read the section on pricing in chapter 4 and then price each of your sample box menus individually, remembering to include everything from the salt to the corkscrew.

*Costing check list*

*Ingredients*
Do not forget to include flavourings and small quantities.
*Utensils*
Greaseproof paper, foil, tubs, shrinkwrap and labels.
*Incidentals*
Salt and pepper, mustard, sugar, milk; hand fresheners.
*Special items*
Corkscrews and napkins, bottle openers, novelties.
*The box*
Plus any string, ribbon, Cellotape or cloths.
*Fuel*
Cooking and/or deliveries.
*Business overheads*
Stationery, telephone, publicity etc.
*Your time*
Keep a record of time spent.
*Profit*
X%

If you are using any returnable items, make sure that you get a deposit for them; people are much more careful with things they know they will have to pay for. If you are catering for a VIP business outing where a deposit might not be appropriate, or as effective since the guests are not paying the bill, you should agree with the client that his company will foot the bill for any loss.

## MAKING UP THE BOXES

Although the food is obviously very important, the incidental items which go into your boxes can make the difference between success and failure. Wine and no corkscrew, ham and no mustard, or coffee and no sugar could all be major disasters. Get these items right,

and maybe add one or two items which are not essentials but are extremely useful, and you will be well on the way to establishing a reputation for first-class service.

## *Picnic Box Check List*

The main dishes (starters, main course, dessert and cheese)
Bread, biscuits and butter
Salt, pepper and other appropriate seasonings
Mustard, tomato ketchup or other sauces
Sugar for fruit, dessert or coffee
Plates, cups and glasses
Knives, forks and spoons
Bread knife or pie knife

145

Corkscrew, bottle or can opener
Hand and face fresheners
Napkins
Tablecloths

Very often clients will provide their own drinks, but you may be expected to provide glasses, corkscrew etc. If you are to provide hot drinks, remember to include the cost of thermos flasks in the deposit.

Even with an extensive check list it is still quite easy to leave things out of individual boxes. To overcome this problem, set up a simple production line. Arrange the boxes in long rows and put in each item on the menu and check list into all the boxes one at a time. In this way you are sure that all the boxes contain say, the starter before you put in the main course.

## GETTING IN THE BUSINESS

Start off by looking at the check list of possible sources of business and, where possible, put some names to the list. Then read the section on 'getting in the business' in chapter 4.

In the 'business' section of your list, one obvious method of getting your services known is by a direct approach to people who may be organising meetings and special events. In the case of meetings, this is usually the senior secretaries of the company, particularly the secretaries of the sales and personnel managers. So find out their names and address your letters directly to them. Make the point in your letter that your services can help to make their lives a lot easier.

For conferences and special events, a direct approach to the Managing Director, Sales Director or the Personnel or Public Relations Manager would probably be most effective. Here, the emphasis should be on first-class food and a service which will help to enhance the image of the company in front of special customers or the press.

In the private sector, local advertising could be useful. However, a closer association with the type of event you are likely to be catering for would probably give better results. Try advertising in the programmes of local sporting events or shows, or get the secretaries of appropriate clubs to post details of your service on the club notice boards prior to major events. Members of a tennis or golf club, for example, are likely to be interested in local tournaments, young farmers clubs in agricultural shows and pony clubs in horsey events.

Another idea is to use a form of direct mail which will get to people interested in such events. Have some small sheets or leaflets giving details of your service printed cheaply and distribute them to people in the car park at the local race course, horse show, or tennis tournament, or place them on car windscreens . If you can pick out your local car registration numbers, so much the better.

Your own boxes are also an excellent place for advertising. You will probably find that much of your business comes from personal recommendation. Once you have established the most useful sizes of boxes, have them over-printed with the name of your service and the address and telephone number. Or have a small card or tiny leaflet printed instead and place it in every lunch or picnic box that leaves your kitchen. Hopefully this will be kept by customers for future reference.

The quality of your food and the efficiency of your service are the salient factors in 'by word of mouth' recommendations. However, the odd touch of originality can certainly help people to remember you and your service. Find out the colour of the client's car for an 'out of the boot' picnic and colour-match the napkins, wrappings, plastic and paper items. The same idea could be applied to a company VIP gathering. Most companies have a special colour which is used for letterheads, van sign writing and the like; find out what this is and match it.

Another way to get your name remembered might be to include details of the event and the people taking part in it. This information can usually be obtained from the organiser's press office, and they may even be prepared to give you leaflets or programmes at a reduced rate.

But whatever clever ideas you come up with, do make sure that they are not carried out at the expense of the rest of your service. A consistently high standard of service will keep your customers coming back for more far longer than any publicity gimmick.

# 13

# Cooking for Dinner Parties

You can start cooking for dinner parties straight away. You do not necessarily need to invest much money, and provided that you are confident in your cooking ability you can join an agency or put a card in the local butcher's or baker's window, and away you go.

Of course, you are not limited simply to dinner parties. Small-scale catering can take in luncheon parties, small buffets and cocktail parties. You yourself will probably decide on the numbers you think you can happily cater for. Most of the cooks I talked to were prepared to cater for up to about twenty for sit-down luncheons and dinners and up to fifty for buffets and canapés. But the average numbers catered for were around 12–14 for sit-down meals and 20–30 for parties.

## GETTING OFF THE GROUND

As with any other money-making venture, it is sensible to sit down and work out exactly what you want to do and the best way of going about it. You should certainly read the section in chapter 3 how to deal with money, and unless you are going to cook exclu-

*'Kitchen? Up the long gallery, through the ballroom, second on the left through the knights' chamber . . .'*

sively in other people's kitchens you should also read the section on legal requirements in the same chapter.

## Agency Work

It is possible in some large towns and cities to join an employment agency specialising in catering staff and they will find work for you. All you will need to do is to take your favourite knife, an apron and any special equipment you need and go along to the client's address to do the cooking. You may also be required to do the shopping.

However, agency work has its drawbacks. You are dependent upon the agency for your flow of work and, of course, they take a sizable percentage of the fee.

## Working for Yourself

Catering for dinner parties on your own can be dove-tailed with a freezer service or a cake decorating service to make a full-time operation, or it can fit in very well with running a home. A number of cooks I know have worked out a very good method of doing part of the cooking in their own kitchens and the rest of it at the client's home. The ratio will depend upon what you find convenient and on how far away you are from the client's house. City cooks often do not have far to go and can take a good deal of the food in a semi-prepared state, while one Devon cook I spoke to made some of the more elaborate desserts in advance but cooked everything else on the premises. Her average journey was a good two or three times that of her London counterpart.

Another advantage of working for yourself is that you will pick up business from those hostesses who want to appear to have done all the cooking themselves. Some of these ladies prefer you to prepare everything in your house and simply deliver it. They will carry out the finishing-off processes themselves.

Cooking for dinner parties requires quite a high standard of cooking. It may be that the hostess has hired outside help because she doesn't have time to cook the meal herself, but a dinner party is, by definition, a special occasion and so she is also looking for something a little above the average. A Cordon Bleu or French cookery course is useful, but by no means essential.

The ability to present the food attractively is very important. Food may be well cooked, but if it is well presented it gains a great deal.

To be successful, you should also be quite unflappable. In my experience, hostesses have a distinct tendency to panic even though, or maybe because, they are not actually doing anything! So you must remain calm and not be rushed into doing something at the wrong time.

## Equipment

A well-equipped kitchen at home will be a great help. Food processors and other gadgets can help to cut preparation time and you may need to take some of the equipment with you to the client's home. I remember turning up at one beautifully appointed kitchen only to find that the owner can hardly have used it! There was no rolling pin. Dazzled on my exploratory visit by the sparkling array of electrical equipment, I had assumed the presence of smaller items. After some thought, I resorted to a well-washed bottle of claret, hoping that it would not be required until it had had time to settle again!

A successful dinner party cook I spoke to in the Midlands has built up over two years a very respectable collection of crockery and she finds that she needs to use it quite regularly. It consists of a dinner service for twenty people plus a wide variety of serving plates and bowls. She also earns a little extra money by charging for its hire. After all, the client would probably have to pay more to hire from a specialist company and the charge also helps to ensure that nothing goes missing. The problem of 'lost' equipment can be quite serious. Another successful cook told me that she will not deliver food in ramekins unless she knows the client well or is staying to serve and clear away.

## Getting Going

Finding the first few clients can be a nail-biting period so read the sections in chapter 1 on market research and in chapter 4 on promotion and advertising. The choice of promotional methods will depend to a large extent on where you live. A door-to-door mailing, for example, could work very well in a wealthy city suburb, but you can hardly trail round all the larger houses in a rural area. Here, a local newspaper advertisement might be a better bet.

National magazine advertising worked very well for some London and Manchester cooks, but my Devon friend got much of her business from a small poster on the golf course notice board. One of the problems with national magazine advertising is that you are at the mercy of other advertisers and the 'phone can start to ring not with new business but with salesmen seeking business from you.

When I started up I was lucky enough to get a write-up in the editorial columns of *The Lady* and though this did not bring in immediate business, it did give rise to a steady stream of clients, some of whom I am sure must have picked up the magazine in their dentist's waiting room months later. So it is worth writing to county and even national magazines with details of your service. The secret is to try to make your operation sound different from everyone else's!

## CHOOSING THE MENU

Much of the business you will be handling will come in at fairly short notice and, on the whole, the client will want to discuss the menu with you there and then. This means that you do not necessarily need to have a list of set dishes or menus as you can plan each job quite separately.

In practice, you will probably find that it is better to have some ideas already on paper. Because the client wants to decide on a menu at once, you will not have much time in which to think up ideas and you will have to reel off the names of suitable dishes on the spot. If you have not thought about it in advance, the forced spontaneity could lead to the suggestion of dishes which are lengthy to prepare or which are not really suitable for your style of catering. You could also get the costing quite wrong by suggesting in an expansive moment a dish with a cost that is way outside your usual range. It is far preferable to have ready a list of possible dishes, all of which fit into your price range and which you can suggest as appropriate. With luck you will be able to make up a complete menu from your list, and, at worst, you will only have to think up one new dish to fit the customer's requirements.

A menu list still allows you to be flexible. You can structure it so that the price depends upon the dishes chosen or organise it in two sections with a reasonably priced and a more expensive menu. You can also indicate which dishes can be delivered and left for the hostess to finish off and which require you be there to finish off. You only need to glance at the list to have a load of excellent ideas at your fingertips.

A good tip is to try and push the dishes that you are making for another dinner at around the same time. If they are accepted you can make the whole lot all at once.

A menu list can be sent out to those clients who want to take their time choosing the meal. Remember that you will need to change the list from time to time to allow for seasonal variations in price, rising prices and to give regular customers a new selection from which to choose.

In putting a list together think about the following factors:

### You Own Personal Choice
Try to cook those dishes which you always do well and which you enjoy making. Add to your repertoire by trying out dishes at special family dinners or at your own dinner parties. When you are confident of the dish, add it to your next list.

### Cost of the Dish
Make sure that the dishes on the list are either well categorised or are roughly around the same price. A potential customer may be attracted to an exotic dish only to find that it is way beyond the amount he or she intended to pay.

### Preparation Time
A dish that takes a long time to prepare or cook contains hidden costs in terms of your time or the amount of fuel used. Also some dishes may not be suitable for leaving with the client to finish off.

Sometimes detailed instructions are simply not enough; you need to be there yourself to ensure the success of the dish. If you think that instructions will be sufficient, test them out on a friend first and see if there will be any difficulties.

## Popular Dishes

Some dishes are always popular and, though you might not choose them yourself, you ought to include a sprinkling in your list. See what is on the menu whenever you go out to eat and if a dish appears regularly maybe you should think about including it on your own list.

## Unusual and Original Dishes

It is a good idea to include one or two very unusual-sounding dishes on the list. They will probably not be chosen very often but they can serve to show that your scope is wider than the general run of dishes. Do be sure that you carry them off successfully if they are chosen!

# Sample Menu

The following sample list gives dishes where the price is dictated by the dishes chosen. Your *own* list will probably have the price by the side of each dish so that you can quote quickly, but the client's copy will merely give a base price, for example, menus from £8 per head.

*Starters*
Sweetbreads in Mustard and Cream Sauce
Carrot and Orange Soup
Tomatoes stuffed with Scrambled Eggs and Smoked Salmon
Avocado Bisque
Salmon Mousseline
*Fougère Scallops
Shrimp Ramekins
French Farmhouse Pâté

Smoked Trout Mousse
Stuffed Smoked Salmon Horns
Courgettes Vinaigrette
*Spinach Soufflé

*Main courses*
Traditional Steak and Kidney Pie
Roast Veal with Lemon Sauce
*Beef Wellington
Boned Leg of Lamb with Peaches and Cauliflower
Coq au Vin
Medallions of Pork with Spinach Stuffing
Chicken Shrewsbury
Roast Duck with Black Cherry Sauce
Lambs Kidneys Dijonaise
Ham with Apricots in Puff Pastry
*Aubergine Tournados with Red Wine Sauce
*Poached Salmon with Hollandaise Sauce

*Vegetables*
Potato Gratin
Roast Potatoes with Herbs
Celeriac/Artichoke and Potato Purée
Parsley Potatoes
Breton Carrots
Peas with Leeks and Herbs
Baked Courgettes
Stuffed Tomatoes
Spiced Red Cabbage
Braised Celery
Mixed Salad in Season
French Bean Salad

*Desserts*
Fresh Raspberry Ice Cream Bombe

*The starred items require personal attention and cannot be left for the hostess to finish off on her own.

Lime and Ginger Ice Cream
Crème Brûlée
Chocolate Pots
Orange Mousse
Old-fashioned Tipsy Pudding
French Apple Pie
Choux Pastry and Gooseberry Ring
Apricot Meringue Gâteau
Fruit Salad in Season
Cheeseboard with Home-baked Breads
Devils on Horseback

The basic price usually includes the shopping, preparation and delivery of the food plus items such as bread and butter. Coffee is often extra, and here some cooks offer an all-in price to include chocolates or homemade petit fours. A slightly higher price is quoted for cooking and dishing up in the client's house and for washing up and clearing away.

## Checking Things Out

It is important to establish early on in the initial discussion exactly how much service the client requires and how much she wants to spend. You can then steer her towards those items which best fit the bill.

If the requirement is for you to attend, you will need to check the timing of the event, what the kitchen is like and whether or not he or she wants the food serving.

*Questions to ask*
1. What time is the dinner to be served? Work out the amount of time it will take you to set things up and from this you can agree your time of arrival.
2. What sort of cooker does the client have? Is it gas or electric? Is there a microwave oven?

3. Are there certain pieces of equipment which you may require, such as a food processor or electric blender?
4. Does the client have sufficient crockery and serving dishes? Take care over the latter; very often clients glibly say that they have plenty of dishes and when you get there you find that they are too few and too small.
5. How is the service to be organised? It is important to make sure that you are not expected to wait at table as well as working in the kitchen. The usual practice is for you to arrange the food on serving plates and the host and hostess will serve their guests. Alternatively, a more formal occasion may demand a waitress or a butler and waitress.
6. Are there likely to be any food problems with vegetarians or foreign guests?
7. Are you to organise the drinks? If so, discuss the wines with the client and check your wine merchant's catalogue for prices, adding on a percentage for your work.
8. Does the client want a full dinner or will she organise vegetables, bread and butter and coffee herself?
9. Are special items such as pre-dinner cocktail canapés or petit fours required?

## SETTING THE PRICES

It is obviously very important to set the prices at the right level. There is no point in setting your prices so high that no one will buy but, on the other hand, you want to earn as much as you can. Prices, therefore, will depend upon the costs involved in producing the meal and upon how much you think people in your catchment area will be prepared to pay.

The first step is to read the section on how much to charge in chapter 4. Next, decide on a list of possible dishes. Cost out all these dishes to the nearest penny. This should not be too onerous as you are not likely to have more than about fifty dishes on offer at any one time. Make sure that you have included an allowance for fuel, stationery and other overheads.

The next thing to consider is your own time, firstly in terms of preparation before the dinner, and secondly in terms of the time involved on the night – are you just delivering or are you staying to finish off the meal, present it and clear it away? The first time consideration should be added to your calculations on the cost of the dish, and the second will be a flat fee added to the total price of catering the meal.

You should now be able to look at your list of dishes and arrange them into groups of similar cost. These prices, together with that of the overall fee, will give you a price to quote for a particular meal. You should also bear in mind the fact that the preparation time will probably be longer for larger amounts.

If you do use this pricing method, it is useful to check the actual cost of the dishes against your estimates each time. This may give you more accurate figures to quote in future and will alert you to seasonal price fluctuations and to rising prices. These records will also help you to work out how profitable your business is.

When you give a client a quotation do not forget to include any extras such as equipment hire charges, deposits on any special dishes used, or staff hire. Invoices are usually presented on the night, either on delivery of the food or at the end of the evening, and the client is expected to pay there and then.

## PLANNING THE DINNER

Start by making a plan for the dinner. This plan should include some or all the following points:

- Booking necessary staff
- Shopping list for food and drinks
- Timing for any advance preparation
- Check list of things to prepare in your own kitchen

- Check list of everything that needs to be done in the client's kitchen,

*or*

- Instructions so that the client can finish off the meal.
- Check list of everything you will need to take with you, including food and equipment.

The menu below would need several check lists.

Stuffed Smoked Salmon Horns

*

Ham with Apricots in Puff Pastry
Artichoke with Potato Purée
Breton Carrots

*

Gooseberry Choux Ring

### The Shopping List
In addition to all the ingredients for the various dishes, you should include: lettuce and tomatoes to garnish salmon horns; brown bread and butter to serve with the salmon horns; and milk, sugar and coffee.

### Advance Preparation
There is no real need to do very much advance preparation with this particular menu but if you are likely to be very busy on the day of the dinner you could make in advance the stuffing for the Salmon Horns, the Artichoke and Potato Purée and the gooseberry filling for the choux ring.

### Preparation on the Day
This might seem rather an obvious list consisting of the dishes on the menu, but you do have to decide how much you are going to

prepare at home and how much in the client's kitchen.

There are also one or two things which can easily be forgotten. These are even more important if you are going to deliver the food rather than finish off the meal yourself. They include washing the lettuce and cutting the tomatoes in flowers or rosettes for garnish on the Salmon Horns, chopping parsley for garnishing the Artichoke and Potato Purée and the Breton Carrots.

Assuming that you are to finish off the meal yourself and that you have done no advance preparation, your list of items to do at home should be as follows:

1. Make the stuffing for the Smoked Salmon Horns.
2. Wash the lettuce and place in polythene bag.
3. Prepare Ham and Apricots in Puff Pastry to the stage where the parcels are ready to go in the oven.
4. Prepare Artichoke and Potato Purée.
5. Make Choux Ring.
6. Make gooseberry filling for the Choux Ring.

## Check List for Client's Kitchen

The corresponding list for things to be prepared in the client's kitchen are as follows:

1. Cut tomato garnish.
2. Make Smoked Salmon Horns, stuff and arrange on plates with the garnish.
3. Prepare carrots and proceed with the recipe.
4. Bake the Ham with Apricots pastry parcels.
5. Re-heat the Artichoke and Potato Purée.
6. Cut the brown bread and butter.
7. Fill choux ring with gooseberry purée and sprinkle with icing sugar.

There is no reason why you should not prepare the whole dinner in the client's kitchen, and this may be necessary if you have a long way to travel. If this is the case, the advance preparation list comes into its own and the rest of the preparation should be amalgamated into one list. Make sure that you arrange things in the correct order. You do not suddenly want to remember that the tomatoes need cutting just as the first course is to be served.

## Instructions for Finishing-off

If the meal is to be delivered for the client to finish off, it is only sensible to deliver it in as complete a form as possible. With this particular meal, the starter can be completed and covered in shrink wrap to keep it fresh. The vegetables and the Choux Ring can also be completed. This just leaves the Ham with Apricots in Puff Pastry to be baked and the vegetables to be heated through in the oven.

Try to make your instructions as detailed as possible and if you have a typewriter, type them out. Otherwise, use your neatest handwriting. If there is anything at all complicated, ask a friend to try it out first!

## Check List of Things to Take

Obviously all the food must go on this list, and here again it is very easy to forget extra items like the icing sugar for the Choux Ring and the milk for the coffee. Do not rely on your client being able to fill the gap – her pantry may be bare.

The chances are that you are unlikely to have time to go and see the kitchen before you go to do the dinner, so take everything that you will need with you. When you have been once you may be able to cut back the list. Items like graters, potato mashers, rolling pins, wooden spoons and sieves are essential.

You will have checked on serving equipment and crockery requirements with the client but do make sure that this check has been sufficiently detailed. I was caught out on one occasion when I took to a house a large French Apple Pie in the flan tin in which it had been cooked, which seemed a sensible way to protect it. The only trouble was that I had not thought of how I was going to serve it, and the client did not have a flat plate large enough!

Paper napkins should also be on your list. They may not be required but you could have a very grateful customer!

## How Much to Make?

The question of how much to make can be a difficult one for beginners. My advice would be to think of how much a hearty eater might require and gear your quantities to that. No hostess wants to appear mean and if your portions are only just sufficient you may not be re-booked.

On the other hand, don't go overboard. Work out the quantities and stick to them. Take care, too, with items like cheeseboards and fruit bowls. To look good, these need to contain a lot more than will actually be eaten. So specify, in advance, that you will be removing the contents of the board or the bowl at the end of the evening, and avoid them altogether if you are simply delivering the meal.

# COOKING ON THE SPOT

The first thing to remember when you are cooking on the spot is that you are a guest in the hostess's kitchen. Do not be too encroaching but do not be too diffident either.

Establish the ground rules first. Do they have any jobs which must be done in the kitchen during the evening? If you know that the au pair will be making her own supper at 7.00 p.m. you can arrange to accommodate that.

What time is the meal to be served and how are you to communicate with the hostess? After all, neither of you is psychic and she needs to know when everything is ready and you need to know when each course has been eaten. If there is a bell system or if you are working with waitresses the solutions are very simple. But if

not, you will need to work out a signalling system with the hostess.

It is quite a nice gesture, if there is a separate dining room, to clear the drawing room of glasses and ashtrays while the meal is being eaten and to wash these up with the rest of the meal.

Establish in advance the time that you are leaving. You do not want to have to sit around in the kitchen while everyone else relaxes over coffee and liqueurs. It is quite usual for the cook to leave after washing up the dessert things, and if these are not returned to the kitchen when the coffee is served, go anyway.

# EXTRA HELP

From time to time you may find that you need extra help, either because you have a particularly large dinner to cater for or because you have two or three to deliver on the same evening. Very often friends can be pressed into service with the promise of a few pounds in the hand but do be sure that they know what they are doing. Check that they are good cooks or are prepared to act as kitchen maids and do all the time-consuming preparatory jobs like washing vegetables, peeling potatoes and preparing meat for a casserole.

The client may want the dinner to be served at the table. In no circumstances should you consider doing this yourself. Most menus will require your full-time presence in the kitchen and, even if they don't, you are not being paid to do two jobs. So hire a waitress.

For further advice on finding extra help and dealing with butlers and waitresses, read the section on staff in chapter 14.

*'No, no, Mavis, the hostess will do* all *her own clearing away!'*

# 14

# Catering in Quantity

Catering in quantity means running a full-time business, and the business considerations covered in chapter 2 will be more important here than they are for a smaller operation.

You will be dealing with lots of different customers and lots of different suppliers and all these transactions need to be carefully recorded if you are not to get your accounts and records into a horrible mess. So study the section on money and set up your business systems straight away.

You will also be dealing with a large volume of work right from the word go. And it can be hard work! There will be a lot of cooking to be done and a good deal of humping boxes of food from the kitchen to the car and from the car to the catering venue.

You may decide that you need some help with the workload, or that you want to share the responsibility with a friend or ex-business colleague. If it is only another pair of hands you are looking for it is probably better to employ one or two people on a part-time and temporary basis whenever you are extra-busy or have a particularly large event to cater for. This way, you are still in charge and what you say goes. If the worst comes to the worst and you simply do not get on, you can always find someone else to help.

*'Ready?'*

If, however, you want someone to share the responsibilities of the business or someone who will put in as much in the way of creative ideas and hard work as you will, then a partnership or a private limited company may be the answer. But whichever arrangement you go for, do be sure of the person or people you are planning to work with. You must still be able to get on well when things are going wrong or when there is a panic preparing for a particular event.

Running a catering company is not *all* hard work. It can be great fun. My ex-partner and I have had many laughs in the kitchen listening to our waitresses describing the assembled company, or

167

listening to guests who have resorted to the kitchen for a quiet gossip about their friends!

It can also be very rewarding. A hostess who is over the moon about the dinner you have provided, or a starry-eyed bride who thanks you for the best day in her life so far, all make the hard work seem well worthwhile.

# THINKING UP A NAME

If you have decided that you want to trade under a business name (see chapter 4), now is the time to think about it seriously. Once chosen, you will need to use it on everything from your letter-headed paper to your car.

All sorts of names are used in the catering business. Here are a few of the names that I have come across over the last few years. They will show the range of imagination that has been used and perhaps help to spark off an idea for a name of your own. They are in no particular order: Gluttons, London Cooks, Below the Salt, Kathy's Kitchen, Travelling Gourmet, Party Planners, Gastronomique, By Word of Mouth, Chez Maurice, City Caterers, Black Cat Caterers, Top Table, Party Fare, Carvers.

Check your local Yellow Pages to make sure that you have not chosen the same name as another caterer in the area. If you are setting up a limited company, a check will be made to ensure that the name you have chosen has not been registered already.

# INVESTMENT IN THE FUTURE

The changes that you make in your kitchen will depend upon the amount of money you have available at the start. However, it is a good idea to set down exactly what your ideal plan would be, for even if you cannot afford everything now you can always plough your profits back into the business later on.

Consult the Food Hygiene Regulations when you are planning your operation and look at the kitchen check list in chapter 3. Think also about the practicalities of the work you will be doing. Work surfaces and storage space for both unprepared and prepared foods would be high on my list. Catering for a wedding buffet for one hundred, for example, takes up a lot of space in a domestic kitchen.

In large-scale catering the emphasis is on large quantities, and anything that makes life easier when faced with peeling and chopping 6 lbs onions or peeling 12 lbs potatoes is worth considering. Here is a list of kitchen equipment both large and small which may be useful. With the larger electrical items it is sensible to go for the heavy-duty or small catering versions as they are going to have to stand up to much more use than in the average domestic kitchen.

## *Kitchen Equipment*

*Electrical equipment*
  Food mixer with all the attachments
  Food processor
  Microwave oven
  Large blender
  Hand-held whisk and mixer
  Electric carving knife
  Potato peeler
  Deep-fat fryer

*General equipment*
  Egg slicer
  Butter curlers
  Julienne cutter
  Pastry horn shapes
  Pastry boat cases
  Melon and potato baller
  Ice cream scoop
  Fish and other shaped moulds

Parsley and herb mill
Large piping nozzles
Small shaped cutters

### Service Equipment

In addition to kitchen equipment you may find it useful to have some of your own service equipment. The chances are that you will be hiring equipment for large events but you may still want to have your own equipment to make an eye-catching centrepiece. You may also take on some small events where the clients do not have much stuff of their own but where it is not really worth incurring the delivery charges on hired equipment.

Look out for large serving plates and bowls in junk shops or in street markets and remember that things like Victorian bowls and ewers can look most attractive on a buffet table.

### Carrying Equipment

Other equipment which must go on the list and which should have a pretty high priority is carrying equipment of various kinds. Cold boxes, ice bags, meat trays and boxes all come into this category. Large and flat trays are also useful for stacking bowls of food as they prevent one bowl from falling into the other. If the trays are interlocking, so much the better. Keep your eyes open and press into service anything that you think will be useful. I found a particularly large set of filing baskets which fitted easily into the boot of a car and took a variety of dishes on each layer to be particularly practical.

As well as the specialised equipment, remember to start collecting large cardboard boxes just before a big event.

### Office Equipment

You should not forget the office when you are getting equipment together. You will need account books and stationery as well as all the usual bits and pieces like staplers and hole punchers. Desk, typewriter and telephone answering machine should all be considered, and a filing cabinet of some kind is essential. Big box files can help here.

# WHAT ARE YOU GOING TO DO?

*Buffet Meals*
Buffet meals can be eaten either with the fingers or with a fork and usually standing up. This means that the menu must be planned so that the food is easy to eat. It is no good serving chicken on the bone or large slices of meat if the guests have only a fork with which to tackle it.

A buffet is served from one long table and the guests usually queue up and help themselves. This means that there can be terrible congestion if things are not planned properly. There should be at least two points at which the queues can form, preferably more if the numbers are over fifty. If the buffet is a simple one and requires no service at all, you can often use both sides of the buffet table – simply duplicate everything along the length of the table.

Some finger buffets are waitress-served and this can help the congestion problem; other buffets are self-service but the guests return to tables and chairs to eat each course. Here, meat or fish can be cut into portions by serving staff behind the buffet and the guests can use knives as well as forks.

Buffets may be served at private and business functions.

*Private*
Luncheon parties
Pre-theatre parties
Evening parties
Entertaining at sports events
Brunches and barbecues

*Business*
General lunchtime meetings
Press conferences

Sales conferences
Entertaining at sports events
Company parties
Breakfast meetings

The reason for the function could throw up other considerations. A birthday party could mean a special cake, and the hostess may want to cut and serve the cake at a particular time. You will need extra plates, and the waiting staff may be required to pass the cake round.

## Canapés

Canapés are always eaten with the fingers and are served at drinks and cocktail parties. The food is usually passed round by the host and the hostess or by the waiting staff, and should be easy to eat in one or two mouthfuls. Be careful of very crumbly things – your client may not thank you for bits of flaky pastry walked into the carpet – and of food which retains its heat. It is very easy to burn your mouth on hot cheese canapés, for example.

Canapés may be served at the following functions:

*Private*
Lunchtime cocktails
Evening cocktails
Evening drinks parties

*Business*
Lunchtime parties
Early evening parties

It is sensible to establish with your client how long the party is to last. In theory, canapés are simply a snack to prevent the guests from rolling around with the effect of the alcohol, but I have catered for some evening cocktail parties where the guests have stayed for three hours or more and consumed the canapés as though they were not intending to eat until morning.

### Sit-down Meals

There are far fewer restrictions on the menu for a sit-down meal than there are for a buffet but you will still need to bear in mind service requirements and the problems of large-scale catering. The right number of staff in the kitchen and waiting at table will make all the difference to the efficient running of a sit-down meal.

Sit-down meals take in both lunches and dinners and private and business functions.

### Wedding Breakfasts

Wedding breakfasts can take any of the previous three forms, but there are a number of special factors which will need to be taken into consideration. These include the reception of the guests, the speeches and toasts, the cutting of the cake and photography, all of which need to be planned for and details agreed with the host and hostess.

### Children's Parties

These, too, are a law unto themselves. They may take the form of a sit-down tea or they may be outdoor buffets or picnic boxes. Remember that the guests will be children and plan accordingly. After all, their tastes are usually quite different to those of an adult – they do tend to make a little more mess and they are quite uninhibited about liking things which are just good fun.

### Picnics and Things

From time to time a variety of other events may come your way and these can only add interest to your everyday business. On one occasion I was asked to provide a gourmet picnic for an executive coach trip to a rugby international, on another it was a hamper to serve from the back of an estate car at Brands Hatch and on a third it was an outdoor buffet for a shooting party. For tips for this sort of catering have a look at chapter 12, but remember you could be operating on a much larger scale.

## Bringing in the Business

The business that comes your way will depend on your own inclinations, the area in which you are operating and the sort of promotion you have done. Try to think of everyone in your area who might be doing some entertaining and is likely to want outside help. This sort of study could reveal the need for a specialist service right on your own doorstep. Here is a check list to start you off. It includes possible sources of business, who to approach and how.

### Business Possibilities Check List

| Source of business | Type of work | Methods of approach | Whom to contact | Sources of information |
| --- | --- | --- | --- | --- |
| Private Individuals | Luncheons<br><br>Dinners<br><br>General parties<br><br>Children's parties | House-to-house mailing<br><br>Yellow Pages advertising<br><br>Local newspapers and magazine advertising<br><br>Local theatre programme advertising<br><br>Shop and Social Club notice boards<br><br>Car stickers | The householders | Check with estate agents to find the better-off areas |
| | Weddings | As above, plus personal letters | The bride or her father | Local newspaper announcements<br>Local bans |

| | Birthdays and anniversaries | As above plus personal letters | Father, wife or relatives of the person with the anniversary | Local newspaper announcements |
|---|---|---|---|---|
| | Sporting events hampers | As above<br><br>Leave business cards or notices anywhere where people who might be interested are likely to be | The householder | Check the area for race courses, tennis and golf tournaments, etc |
| Private businesses, including insurance companies, trade associations government departments and local governments | Meetings and parties | Personal letters | Any managers who might be organising regular staff meetings, including company secretaries and personnel managers | Yellow Pages<br><br>Check local representatives who might organise social functions as part of their sales efforts |
| | Conferences | Personal letters | Sales managers, public relations managers | |
| | Social events | Personal letters | Social club secretary | |

# FIXED OR FLEXIBLE MENUS?

The next thing to start thinking about is the sort of menus you intend to offer. These need to be thought about pretty early on as they can affect the way you work, and they may also be needed for your promotional material.

There are two schools of thought: you can either discuss each order individually with clients as they contact you or you can work out set lists of dishes and menus. The first method is very flexible but it has certain disadvantages. You must be able to talk off the cuff, at any time, about the sort of food you can offer, and you may need to make quite a few suggestions before hitting on something which appeals to the prospective client.

Unlike dinner hosts and hostesses, who usually want to make up their minds there and then, large-scale clients like to have something to look at before deciding to hire you, and they will not always take the time to give you detailed requirements. This is particularly so if they are considering three or four possible caterers. You can, of course, work out half a dozen menus and send them off, but after you have done this a number of times 'on spec' you will begin to wish that you had a ready-made list to submit.

You will definitely need to have some examples of possible menus if you intend to approach prospective customers by means of a direct mail shot.

The problem, of course, with set menus and lists is not only that regular clients can get bored with them but that they do not take into account seasonal availability, clients with special requirements or, indeed, the fact that you too may get bored preparing the same things all the time.

The answer is probably a combination of both methods. Work out three or four sample menus for the different sorts of business you think you are likely to attract, or prepare a list of dishes to choose from. Update these sample menus and lists every three months or so. At the same time, make it clear in your telephone conversations or correspondence that you like to work to individual requirements and will happily work out a selection of special menus on request.

Sample menus can be duplicated on to letter-headed paper to save expensive printing costs every time you change the menus. Once you are established and have more money to spare for promotional material you might like to design some menu cards and these could be used both to give sample menus and for the event itself.

## PLANNING MENUS

Your menus, and the execution of them, are your showcase and so you must balance what people like and are used to with the need to show originality and flair. Identify the dishes you (and your partner if you have one) are good at making and use these as the basis on which to build up your menus.

Cost is a major consideration and it is useful to have a range of menus which are suitable not only for different types of events but also for different budget levels. The seasonal availability of certain products is also important because the price of some foods can fluctuate tremendously. A strawberry dessert in the summer can be a reasonable proposition but in winter the price will be sky high. Of course, some foods are available frozen out of season but these, too, can be a bit pricey, and strawberries, for instance, are nothing like the same after they have been frozen.

You can get caught out when offering quite simple foods which are suddenly unavailable for a short period. I was happily putting stuffed celery on my canapé menus only to find that celery was all of a sudden totally unavailable. Not too serious in this case – but it could have been.

The workload involved in preparing the menu is a very important factor which may not at first be obvious, particularly if your pricing system does not take total time into account. You may, for example, come up with a summer menu along the following lines:

Salmon and Whiting Terrine

\*

Chicken Kiev with Vegetables

\*

Gooseberry Choux Ring

None of these recipes is particularly onerous in itself but each one needs a fair amount of preparation work. The terrine needs to have the various ingredients cut or minced to different sizes and these must then be arranged in the dish; the chicken must be taken off the bone and stuffed before it is cooked; and the dessert has two parts to its preparation.

Finger buffets and canapés can be time-consuming to prepare. To offer pastry boats, choux balls, canapés set with aspic and stuffed eggs all in the same menu, even with one or two simpler items, is really making work for yourself.

Of course, time does not matter if you are charging sufficient to cover the cost of extra help, but very often this is not the case.

The numbers involved could also affect the sort of menu you would offer. Some dishes are fine for small numbers but can be difficult if you are catering for fifty plus, whereas casseroles and roasts are very easy to cook in quantity. On the other hand, the profit margins on larger events are also greater and so you can afford to offer more time-consuming items.

Finally, the same considerations which apply to the planning of any meal also apply in large-scale catering. The richness of the different dishes, their textures and colour are all important. Nowadays, people are much more careful of what they eat and on the whole they do not want rich dishes in every course. Nor do they want to eat the same sort of thing all the time. To serve all the food either deep-fried or in pastry would not only be nutritionally bad but would be extremely boring.

## Fork Buffets

Texture and colour become very important when you are planning a buffet as all the food is arranged on a table together.

Listed below are some sample buffet menus devised with different price ranges and different types of events in mind.

*Low Cost Menus suitable for a Luncheon Buffet or a Small Informal Party*

*Hot*
> Cream of Watercress Soup
> Coq au Vin with rice and vegetables
> Apple Trifle

*Cold*
> Vichysoisse or Gazpatcho
> Selection cold flans (Chicken and Asparagus, Seafood in Aspic, Egg and Peas)
> Selection of salads
> Gooseberry Fool

*Low Cost Menus suitable for a Large Evening Party Buffet*

*Hot*
> Selection hot stuffed vegetables
> Lemon Chicken with rice and vegetables
> Moccha Cream Pudding
> Fruit Salad, in season

*Cold*
> Pork and Spinach Terrine
> Breton Fish Loaf with Piquant Sauce
> Chicken Waldorf Salad
> Selection of salads
> Apricot Meringue Gâteau
> Pears in Red Wine

*More Expensive Menus suitable for All Types of Events*

*Hot*
    Smoked Trout Pâté with fresh tomato purée
    Beef in Red Wine with vegetables and new potatoes
    Damson Cheesecake
    Fresh Raspberry Mousse

*Cold*
    Mushrooms à la Grecque
    Danish Pressed Beef with Green Bean Salad
    Salmon and Egg Terrine
    Selection of Salads
    Gooseberry Choux Ring

*Hot*
    Chicken and Fennel Cocktail
    Spiced Pork with Oranges, with rice and vegetables
    Black Bottom Pie
    Apple and Berry Pie

*Cold*
    Chilled Avocado Bisque
    Cold Spiced Beef with mixed Ham and Tongue Cornets and
        Stuffed Artichoke Hearts
    Selection of salads
    Stuffed Peaches in White Wine

## Finger Buffets

I am often asked what to include in a finger buffet so rather than set out specific menus I have put together a list of both hot and cold items from which a buffet can be built up. Add your own specialities to the list, but remember to take care not to pick all the complicated items. About six or seven items are usually quite sufficient. Try to visualise all the items you choose set out on one plate and then see if you think they will be enough.

*Hot food*

Small or medium vol-au-vents:
  Filled with mushrooms, chicken, asparagus, egg and peas, ham,
  smoked haddock or curried sauces.

Chicken Drumsticks:
  Seasoned or herbed, coated with flavoured breadcrumbs,
  stuffings, egg and peanuts or crisps.

Baby Lamb Chops:
  As for chicken drumsticks.

Goujons:
  Sole, huss, monkfish, prawns; flavoured, or coated with
  breadcrumbs or breadcrumbs and parmesan.

Pastry Rolls:
  Filled with sausage, savoury mince or fish.

Pastry Pinwheels:
  Tomato, liver pâté, cheese and onion fillings.

Pastry Boats or tartlets:
  Filled with scrambled egg, spiced vegetables, quiche; see also
  vol-au-vents.

Quiche:
  Blue cheese, smoked fish, green pepper and sweetcorn, bacon
  and onion, spinach.

Sausages:
  Cocktail, chipolatas, Viennas with tomato, mustard, piquant and
  barbecue sauces.

Satay:
  Small pieces chicken, lamb or pork on cocktail sticks with peanut
  butter sauce.

Some of the items listed under hot canapés below could be made a little larger and used in a finger buffet.

*Cold food*

Stuffed Eggs:
  Prawns, bean sprouts, smoked salmon, mock caviar, curry fillings.

Stuffed Tomatoes:
  Scrambled eggs, cheese and Russian Salad fillings.

Asparagus Rolls

Sandwich Kebabs

Smoked Brisling Fingers

Some of the items listed under cold canapés below could be made a little larger and used in a finger buffet.

# Canapés

Follow the same principles as for finger buffets but make the items and the quantities smaller. Guests are unlikely to have plates and so most items should be one- or two-bite sized. It is very easy to get the quantities wrong at a drinks party. Five or six items on the canapé menu should be more than enough for business parties starting at 6.00 p.m., while seven or eight would be nearer the mark for Sunday lunchtime cocktails.

*Selection of Hot and Cold Canapés*

*Hot*
Deep Fried Mushrooms:
  Coated in batter served with mayonnaise or tartar sauce.

Meatballs and Fish Balls:
   Served with mustard and tomato-based sauces, tartar sauce or
   curried mayonnaise.

Cheese Dreams:
   Tiny cheese and chutney sandwiches fried in butter, or cheese
   and courgette sandwiches dipped in egg and fried.

Deep-fried Gems:
   These are very thick cheese sauces coated in egg and
   breadcrumbs and deep fried; use a variety of different cheeses.

Deep-fried Puffs:
   These are light batters filled with prawns, smoked fish, grated
   vegetables, chicken or ham.

Angels and Devils on Horseback:
   Prunes, oysters, chicken livers wrapped in bacon and grilled.

Small Pizza Squares

Falafel

Pastry Bites:
   Small strips of pastry wrapped round stuffed olives, cocktail
   gherkins and half pickled walnuts.

Toasted Ham and Tongue Pinwheels

Some of the items listed for finger buffets may be made smaller and
used as canapés.

*Cold*

Choux Pastry Balls:
   Filled with flavoured cream cheese, taramasalata, hummus or
   scrambled eggs.

Cucumber Crowns:
   Cucumber, sliced egg yolk and mock caviar or stuffed olives.

Egg and Shrimp Biscuits or Boats:
Very useful for using up the egg white slices left from making cucumber crowns. Chop and mix with canned or potted shrimps and butter.

Savoury Cheese Truffles:
Mix cheese or cream cheese and fruit balls rolled in spices, toasted sesame seed, ground dried orange rind.

Savoury Cocktail Biscuits or Strands:
Cheese, herb, curry, tomato, peanut flavours.

Stuffed celery, prunes and dates:
Flavoured cream cheese, nuts and cocktail pickles.

Smoked salmon or bacon wrapped round water chestnuts

Dips with crudités:
Use beans, chick peas and tomato purée as alternative base to cheese.

Pinwheel sandwiches

Assorted canapés:
Use fried bread base for a richer effect.

Some of the items listed under cold finger buffet food can also be made in smaller sizes and served as canapés.

## Sit-down Meals

For ideas for sit-down meals look at the suggestions in chapter 13, Cooking for Dinner Parties. But remember that you will have to produce the dishes in much larger quantities.

### Discussing the Menu with the Client
The first thing to establish, whether you are working from fixed menus and lists of specific dishes or whether you are starting from scratch and creating a menu to suit the needs of the client, is the

amount of money he or she wants to spend. There is no point in spending all the client's money on a splendid meal if there is nothing left to pay for proper service.

You need to inquire about any special preferences or requirements that the host or guests might have, the numbers, the timing of the event, details of extra requirements such as pre-dinner canapés or petit fours, and the availability of crockery and cutlery.

### *Questions to Ask Potential Clients*
1. What sort of event is it – dinner, buffet, etc?
2. At what time of the day is the event to be held?
3. How many people are they thinking of inviting?
4. How much is the customer thinking of spending?
5. What sort of food has the client in mind?
6. Are there to be any guests with special dietary requirements?
7. How many courses do they want? At a buffet luncheon, for example, you can get away with serving only two courses, whereas a dinner could run into five or six.
8. Do they want you to do the drinks, and if so what? Do they want a full bar for a party or just wine, or do they want special cocktails?
9. Are pre-meal canapés required?
10. Do they want coffee, and do they want petit fours served with it?

The answers to all these questions will not only affect the choice of menu but also the amount of crockery, cutlery and glass that needs to be hired, the number of staff needed to prepare, serve and clear away the food, and last, but by no means least, the price.

If you do not establish these points in advance you may find yourself having to charge more than your first quote (and no client likes that) or, even worse, you may be left footing the extra bill yourself.

Preliminary discussions are extremely important if you want to make sure that your clients are really pleased with the food. After all, you want them to come back to you again and to recommend you to all their friends.

You may come up against slight problems with some clients who have very definite views. (If every hostess who demanded quiches for her buffet got her way, no one would ever eat anything else!) You must very tactfully try to convince the client that her ideas may not be the best. If you can manage this delicate manoeuvre, it usually pays off with appreciation on the day.

# BE PREPARED

So far, I have only talked about fairly straightforward dinners, buffets and canapés, but you may be faced with all kinds of different requests for special catering. Try to be prepared rather than have to think up an answer on the spur of the moment.

## Wedding Breakfasts

Although the food will be either that for a sit-down meal, a buffet or canapés, there are special considerations to take into account when dealing with a wedding breakfast. Even if the clients do not have vast sums of money to spend, they still want something rather special. There is also wedding protocol to take into account, and special questions to ask.

- How are the guests to be received and what drinks are to be served at this stage?
- Is there to be a cake?
- Is there to be champagne for the toasts?

*Sample Menus*

*Cold*
  Salmon Ring Mousse with Cucumber Sauce
  Avocado Mousse

Herb Stuffed Veal with Lemon Mayonnaise and Watercress
  Salad
Oriental Seafood Salad with Carrot and Banana Salad
Courgette Salad
Tomato and Onion Salad
French Potato Salad

Strawberry Romanoff
Chocolate and Hazelnut Ice Cream Gâteau

*Hot*
Individual Smoked Salmon Pâté Moulds in Aspic with Sour
  Cream Sauce

Lamb in Burgundy
Devilled Kidneys with Madeira
Anna Potatoes
Spinach Gratin
Glazed Carrots

Profiteroles
Fresh Fruit Salad

## Children's Parties

The thing to remember with children's parties is that the food should please the kids and their tastes are likely to be far less sophisticated and even more traditional than the tastes of their parents. Go for savoury rather than sweet things, but if it is a birthday party a cake is a must. Have some extra paper napkins ready so that the children can take some cake home – they are very often too full to eat it at the end of the meal!

Here are some ideas for fun foods to serve. Presentation is important with children. They are much more likely to go for something that looks attractive than for something good but plain.

Also check the section on children's cakes in chapter 9, Celebration Cake Service.

*'Don't be silly, Mary. They're only children!'*

*Children's food*
  Open Sandwich Boats
  Sausage Cannon
  Cheese and Onion Hedgehogs
  Crocodile Surprise Loaf
  Salad and Sandwich Kebabs
  Decorated Burgers
  Roly Poly Sandwiches
  Ice Cream Cabin
  Ice Cream Clowns
  Clock Pudding
  Shaped Jellies

## Vegetarian Food

If you are asked to cater for vegetarians it is important to establish what sort of vegetarians they are. Some will eat fish whereas others have such a strict diet that they will not even eat dairy foods. The latter group are called Vegans and they will not eat anything that comes from an animal source.

Vegetarian food can be just as attractive to look at and delicious to eat as food with meat. Here are some sample menus for fork and finger buffets and canapés – the same considerations on balance of colours, texture and ingredients apply as those discussed earlier.

### *Fork Buffets*

*Hot buffet*
  Individual Jellied Lemon and Cucumber Salads with Sour Cream
  Egg and Artichoke Flan
  Hot Cauliflower Terrine
  Ratatouille
  New Potatoes
  Lemon Tart

*Cold buffet*
  Green Pea Soufflé
  Tarragon Scrambled Egg Flan with Asparagus
  Blue Cheese Quiche
  Ilchester Smoked Cheese Log
  Selection of salads
  Chocolate Choux Ring
  Cinnamon Applecake

### *Finger Buffets (hot and cold)*

*Hot*
  Spiced Lentil Vol-au-vents
  Herbed Potato Puffs

189

*Cold*
  Tarragon and Egg Tartlets
  Curried Bean and Onion Croûtes
  Mixed Choux Puffs
  Stuffed Tomatoes
  Selection of Baby Open Sandwiches
  Cheese and Carrot Stuffed French Loaf
  Savoury Cheesecake Squares

*Canapés (hot and cold)*

*Hot*
  Falafel
  Camembert Gems

*Cold*
  Mali Canapés
  Stuffed Dates with Almonds
  Sesame Truffles
  Mixed Brown Toast Canapés
  Peanut and Garlic Dip
  Piquant Cheese Dip with crudités

There are one or two hidden pitfalls which you will need to remember when catering for strict vegetarians. Gelatine, for example, comes from an animal source, but you can substitute agar agar or gelozone. Stock cubes, Worcestershire sauce and some ready-made pastries are not suitable, and you will need to look for rennet-free cheese.

## Jewish Food

Orthodox Jews are unlikely to ask you to do their catering unless you, too, keep a strict kosher kitchen. However, there are plenty of Jewish people who do not keep *all* the dietary rules and are only concerned about a few basic principles – and many of them will use non-Jewish caterers.

You need to know that the Jews differentiate between three categories of foods: meat foods, dairy foods and neutral foods which include fish, eggs, fruit and vegetables. The first two must not be eaten together at the same meal, though the last, neutral, group can be eaten with either of the other two. This often means that a Jewish hostess will keep meat and dairy foods apart in a particular dish but will serve both types of dishes at a party, leaving it to the individual guest to decide whether to stick to one type or the other or to eat both.

There are some foods which Jewish people do not eat at all. These include pork, rabbit, hare, leg of lamb and all kinds of shellfish. Strictly speaking, the meat should have come from animals which have been slaughtered in a special way, so check with your hostess to find out if she wants to have kosher meat.

## PRICING YOUR MENUS

First of all read the section on how much to charge in chapter 4 and then apply it to your menus. Cost each dish separately. Your initial costs could include some or all of the following incidental items, which can easily be forgotten:

Paper napkins
Candles
Flowers
Aluminium foil
Shrink wrap
Menu cards
Coffee, milk and sugar
Bread and butter

Keep a note of your estimated prices and then check the real costs against the estimates. This is very good exercise for improving your estimating abilities, and it ensures that you notice rising costs as they happen rather than a few weeks later.

Include an indication of hire and staff costs with your menu prices so that the client can see exactly how much the total will be. A client is unlikely to take very kindly to an unexpected bill for equipment hire.

With your estimate set out your terms of business. Where possible, try to cover your costs in advance. (This is a great help in avoiding cash flow problems.) I usually ask for 50% of the food costs in advance, payable on confirmation of the numbers. I then invoice the remainder together with any other costs either on the day of the event or directly afterwards.

# VISITING THE VENUE

If you are planning to cook the whole meal on the premises or if a very large party is planned, it is a very good idea to go and have a look at the venue.

## *The Kitchen or Food Preparation Area*

- Check the general layout, working surface area and the need for extra trestle tables to work at.
- What appliances are available and how do they work? Ask now when the hostess has some time rather than on the day when she may be a little rushed. For some venues you may need to hire hotplates or cooking equipment.
- How much small equipment is there? This includes things like pans and kitchen utensils. Make a list of what you will need to take yourself.
- Check the electric points. Some old buildings still have old-fashioned plugs and if you are taking your own equipment you do want to have the correct plugs.
- Check the availability of fridge space to chill food and wine.
- Is there a second sink unit or outside sink for chilling the wine? If not, could you use a dustbin?
- Check the washing up arrangements. How much space is there?

- How far is the kitchen from the service area? This could affect the number of staff required.
- As a result of this check, will you need to do more preparation in advance?

*Service Areas*
- Check the placing of the buffet table or the tables and chairs. Is there enough space for the proposed numbers and for the service? Do the tables and chairs need to be hired?
- What is the colour scheme of the rooms? This is obviously important for the selection of the colours for napkins, candles and flowers.
- Where is the bar to be placed? Is there enough room?
- For weddings, you will need to check where the guests are to be received and the subsequent drinks service as well as the placing of the tables and chairs.

*Bathrooms and Toilets*
- Check where these facilities are situated so that you can pass the information on to waiting staff. They, in turn, will be able to answer guests' inquiries.

*The client*
- Agree the details of the equipment to be hired.
- Make sure that the client understands and agrees to your terms of business. Agree a cut-off date for final numbers. Five working days should give you enough time to prepare for even very large events.

# PLAN OF CAMPAIGN

You should now be in a position to make out a complete plan of campaign for the event. This is important as there are dozens of things that could so easily be forgotten.

*Party Plan of Campaign*
1. Order all hire equipment by telephone. Confirm in writing, giving name and address of venue and your own name and address for the bill.
2. Book all staff and discuss their transport arrangements.
3. Make out a plan for the preparation of all the dishes, indicating those which can be made in advance and those which must be made on the day.
4. Make out complete shopping lists for all the food, wine and incidentals. Organise these into an advance shopping list and one for the day before.
5. Do the advance shopping.
6. Do the advance preparation.
7. Make a check list of all the things you will need to take with you, including the prepared dishes, the unprepared food, equipment and incidentals.
8. Make a check list of things to be done at the venue, including decoration of food and checking equipment hire.
9. Plan the method of transport to the venue, with a fall-back plan in case the transport breaks down.
10. Confirm by telephone the catering equipment hire and delivery, and any other items such as the wine or the cake.
11. Buy the food for final preparation and plan where to buy ice on the day.
12. Complete final food preparation.
13. Prepare the invoice.
14. Bring records up to date.

It is very important to book the catering hire equipment and the staff as soon as possible. At certain times of the year, such as Christmas and the summer months, everyone wants these facilities and you could have a problem if you leave arrangements to the last minute.

If you have any doubts about obtaining a particular ingredient, shop for it in good time or ring round likely suppliers to see if it is available.

When you come to put a time estimate on the shopping and food preparation do allow more time than you think you will need. I inevitably underestimate the time required for such jobs and I have been at it for six or seven years!

A final word of warning: however good the facilities at the venue appear to be, you should still plan to do as much as possible in advance. Unfamiliar equipment and layout make for delays. The staff will also keep interrupting you with requests for guidance and the host or hostess may also keep popping in and out of the kitchen.

Keep your check lists for different types of events and look at them after each event to see if you should have added anything else.

# HIRING EQUIPMENT

Unless the event is a very small one you will need to hire glasses, crockery and cutlery as well as serving plates and trays, and the list may be extended to include items like linen tablecloths and napkins, candlesticks, flower vases, and even tables and chairs.

There are specialist companies in most large towns that will hire out anything from a bottled gas cooker to a silver punch bowl and it is a good idea to get to know your local companies as soon as possible. Have a look in the Yellow Pages under Catering Equipment Hire.

Check them out to see what sort of service they can offer. How far will they deliver and how much does it cost? Do they have pretty crockery or is it all plain white? What is the cutlery like? Do they have specialist equipment? Are they reliable?

Once you have found a company which you think is satisfactory, stick with them. If you can, build up a good working relationship with your hire company as they may help to get you out of a last-minute crisis one day.

Make a list of the equipment that will be needed as early in the planning stages as possible and get it booked. Do not forget small items like cruets, sugar bowls and milk jugs. Here is a sample check list for a wedding breakfast.

*Equipment hire check list*
    Side plates for bread and butter
    Medium plates for the starter (cocktail dishes or soup bowls)
    Dinner plates
    Dessert plates or bowls
    Side knives
    Knives and forks for the starter (teaspoons or soup spoons)
    Knives and forks for the main course
    Dessert spoons and forks
    Serving spoons and forks
    Serving plates
    Trays for the drinks
    Large serving bowls
    Cruets
    Coffee cups and saucers
    Coffee spoons
    Coffee pots, milk jugs and sugar bowls
    Glasses for reception drinks
    Wine glasses
    Champagne glasses
    Table vases
    Ashtrays
    Candlesticks
    Table cloths
    Napkins
    Two trestle tables for the buffet
    Tables and chairs and hotplates if needed.

Obviously the equipment needed for a finger buffet would be a lot less. One point to remember here is that the serving plates should not be too big. Once they are loaded with food they can be very heavy for the waitresses to carry through the crowd.

    If you do not have much help you can often save on the washing up by sending the equipment back unwashed. However, most hire companies charge considerably more if they have to wash up dirty glasses, crockery and cutlery.

# DEALING WITH STAFF

Once you start catering for twenty or more you are going to need extra help either in the kitchen or for serving food.

If you ask friends to help you, make sure that their help is organised on a businesslike basis, with a certain amount of money agreed for a certain amount of time, and establish that you are boss.

I have found that unskilled help is best in the kitchen. This way you get all the laborious and dirty jobs done, plus the washing up, leaving you free to do the skilled work and to concentrate on presentation.

Professional help is essential 'front of the house' and in the service area. An experienced butler or head waitress really can be worth his or her weight in gold. Listen to their advice and you will learn a lot about presenting, managing and serving food.

If you are running a partnership or a limited company with a number of you involved together, it is tempting to try and make a little extra money by acting as your own waiting staff. This can be quite fun once or twice and will certainly show you what the waiting staff have to put up with, but it tends to create an amateurish impression. I also doubt if you would want to do it more than a few times – it is amazing how rude some people can be to those who are serving them.

Finding good staff can be difficult at first so do make a note of anyone you find who is good. There are staff agencies you can contact, and you can also advertise in the local paper. Staff do not always have their own cars and so you will either have to pay for a taxi to and from inaccessible venues or arrange for them to be picked up and returned to a central point.

### How Many Waitresses?

The number of serving staff required will depend on the number of guests and on the type of event.

*Sit-down Meals*
Here you will need one waitress for up to 12 people. The waitresses will set the tables, organise the service area, wait at table and help wash up. Extra staff will be needed if there are drinks to be served before the meal or if there are a number of different wines to be served with the meal. If the numbers are large you will also need help with the service in the kitchen.

For a very formal event a butler will be invaluable for he will oversee everything that is happening outside the kitchen and will organise barman, waiters and waitresses.

*Fork Buffet*
This type of meal probably needs the fewest staff. Guests help themselves and the organisation is much simpler. However, with large numbers, waitresses will be needed to set up and serve behind the buffet, to serve the drinks and to clear the tables or surrounding surfaces. And there is still the washing up! Numbers of staff will depend on the number of guests. Allow at least one waitress to 25 people.

*Finger Buffets and Canapés*
The cold food is usually left on the buffet table or scattered around the room but the hot food does need to be handed round and the drinks need to be served. You may need help in the kitchen as hot food may have to be finished off at the last minute. Here again, numbers will depend on the number of guests; allow two waitresses to thirty guests.

*Wedding Breakfasts*
You are likely to need more waitresses for a wedding buffet than

for a normal buffet or sit-down meal. There are usually more drinks to be served, such as champagne with the toasts, and there is the cake to be cut and handed round.

Whether you have a single waitress or a bevy of waitresses with a barman and butler, it is most important to brief them well. They need to know exactly what is happening and when, where everything is and what their duties are. If one member of staff is in charge, make sure you pass any order through him or her. If there is no time to do this, make sure you give them their instructions as soon as possible.

### Tipping

The question of tipping is not always an easy one. If the client hands over a tip for the staff then you pass it on, but very often clients do not think about it. It is a good idea to cost in an average tip for the staff and then decide on the day how much to give on the basis of how well the job has been done.

# BUYING AND PREPARING FOOD AND DRINK

Discounts for bulk buying of food can be well worth having and they are covered in chapter 1.

## Setting Up a Bar

Buying and serving wine is fairly straightforward. It can very often be bought by the case (12 bottles) on a sale or return basis. This means that you simply charge for what is consumed and return the rest to the supplier.

A full bar can be a little more difficult. You will need stocks of the following drinks: whisky, vodka, gin, rum, brandy, dry and sweet vermouth, Dubonnet, sherry, wine and beer. With this selection you should be able to cater for most preferences as well as for a selection of popular cocktails. In addition, you will need a good stock of soft drinks and mixers. These should include soda water, dry ginger ale, bitter lemon, tonic water, fruit juices and squashes.

Predicting the quantities can be difficult. They will depend on the size of the drinks served, the length of the party and the mood of the guests. However, assuming you serve 1 oz of spirit per drink you will get 26 drinks from the average bottle of spirits. You will find that gin and whisky will be much more popular than the others.

Martini and sherry will require 2–3 oz per glass, bringing the bottle yield down to eight to ten glasses. Allow five glasses from a bottle of wine.

## Preparation in Advance

I like to prepare as much food in advance as possible, but not *too* far in advance. Unless you are absolutely sure of the job, it could be cancelled or the numbers could be drastically cut. If you ask for the final numbers five working days in advance this should give you enough time to do the preparation work.

If you are working more than a couple of days in advance you will need to think very carefully about the storage of the food. Will it all go in the fridge or larder? Remember that the Food Hygiene Regulations require meat products to be kept below 50°F/10°C.

The freezer can be the answer for some foods. Provided that you are careful and follow the freezer manufacturer's instructions, it is permissible to freeze food for use in a subsequent sit-down meal or buffet. Thaw at the last minute as food which has been frozen seems to spoil more quickly. Freezing can affect the texture of some foods. I never freeze those inevitable quiches, for example, as the pastry always seems to go soggy and the fillings stiffen up. However, uncooked pastry dishes freeze very well.

Some items, like bread, cakes and casseroles, are totally unaffected by freezing. You should sort out the dishes you are planning to make according to the ease of storage. Cook the freezable ones first, then the ones that can be refrigerated, and lastly those which need to be stored in tins or in the open larder. Don't forget that cooked pastry seizes up in the fridge, and that other items including cold meats, cheese, butter, ice creams and sorbets will need to be taken out of the fridge or freezer to soften up.

## How Much to Make?

This is always a tricky question, both for the inexperienced and the experienced cook. You do not want to run out of food, nor do you want to over-cater and waste your profits. You will probably find that your client is no help – she is probably encouraging you to panic and prepare too much.

The answer is to sit down and work out the quantities from smaller amounts within your experience. You know how much is required for four, six or even eight people. So start to double up making allowance at 50, 100, 150 and 200 for the overestimating you probably did at the beginning. A small amount left over or served as 'seconds' for eight people will have grown to at least five or six portions on 50 people, and so on.

Start converting your recipes on the doubling up principle, then check after you have used them for the first time to see if the quantities were correct. If not, adjust them. Some ingredients may not need to be increased quite as much as others. This applies to strong flavourings and to the liquid and thickening ingredients.

It is quite a chilling thought that everything you throw away is profit thrown away; though this may not be strictly true, it will help you to think of ways of saving food. Never waste breadcrusts for example, make them into breadcrumbs and store in the freezer. The same applies to leftover cheese from the cheeseboard which can also be grated and stored in the freezer.

## Final Check List

The night before the event is probably the time to sit down and make a list of everything you need to take with you. The list of equipment will vary according to the amount of equipment available at the venue. But really the golden rule is to take everything you think you will need with you. Believe it or not, I did a party at one private house and found that there was no salt and pepper on the premises!

## Wedding Breakfast Check list

This check list is for the cold wedding breakfast suggested on pages 186–187. It lists the foods that can be prepared in advance and the ingredients that are needed to complete the dishes.

| *Prepared food* | *Ingredients* |
|---|---|
| Salmon Ring Mousse | Cucumber and sour cream for sauce |
| Avocado Mousse | |
| Stuffed Veal Lemon Mayonnaise | Watercress and dressing for salad |
| Oriental Seafood Salad | Dressing for salad Carrots and bananas for salad |
| | Courgettes and dressing for salad |
| | Tomatoes and onion for salad |
| Cooked potatoes | Dressing for salad |
| Meringue for Romanoff | Strawberries and cream for Romanoff |
| Chocolate and Hazelnut Ice Cream Gâteau | |
| Bread and butter (brown and French) | |

| *Other items* | *Kitchen equipment* |
|---|---|
| Salt and pepper | Sharp knife |
| Cream | Carving knife |
| Sugar | Knife to cut the cake |
| Milk | Grater |
| Coffee | Sieve |
| Candles | Spoons and forks |
| Napkins | Chopping board |
| Ice (plenty) | Mixing bowls |
| Wine | Bottle opener |
| Drinks and soft drinks | Corkscrew |
| Lemons and cocktail | Binliners |
| cherries | Teatowels |
| | Aprons |

# DELIVERING THE FOOD

You will probably be delivering your own food, but if you get very busy it is possible that you will have more than one event to cater for on one day. One caterer I know has a small team of helpers who simply pick up the food – perhaps a cold lunch buffet or party canapés – and deliver it to the venue, and sometimes they stay and set up the buffet and supervise the waitresses.

In either case you must be sure of the competence of your helpers. Take them with you to start with so that they can see how you do things. Later put them in charge of an event but go along yourself just to make sure that they really know what they are doing. Only then should you send them out by themselves. It is also a good idea to let your client know what is happening as he or she will be used to seeing you in person. Check afterwards that everything was up to standard.

Whether you are delivering the food yourself or are leaving it to a helper, make a list of everything you are taking with you and check it off on return. This is even more important if the food is being left for the client to see to alone. Very often empty dishes are left in an office block foyer overnight for you to collect the next day and this is when things can disappear.

I once had a case of wine 'walk' when I was delivering to a large office block. I had gone up to the venue with a lift-full of food and equipment and when I returned to get the rest the case had gone. Make a point of asking the commissionaire or receptionist to keep an eye on anything that you have to leave for a while.

One answer to the problem of carrying heavy things for a fair distance from a car park to a venue is to invest in a trolly. Put some thought into this purchase as some of the items you will want to transport may be a little awkward to stack. However, boxes and mealtrays will take most things and can be stacked with trays between them to stop one box slipping inside another and thus crushing the food.

It is very important to protect the food while it is in transit, which means covering it up as well as protecting it from knocking and crushing. Shrink wrap is invaluable, and so, for some jobs, are foil and good old-fashioned greaseproof paper.

Do try to arrive in good time for the event – for your client's peace of mind rather than yours! You know that there is only a certain amount to do but your client is usually inclined to believe that there is a mountain of setting up to be done. It is not good for business if your client is in a state of panic when you arrive, for even if things go perfectly he or she is more likely to remember the panic than anything else. Allow plenty of time for traffic delays, and if you are not sure how long the journey is likely to take, do a dummy run at the same time of the day a few days or a week before.

## ACTION ON THE SPOT

This is the time to consult your check list of things to be done on the spot. The check list for the wedding on pages 186–187 would look something like the following:

*Venue Check List*
- Final timing check with host and hostess, if there.
- Check the hire equipment against the inventory.
- Put wine/champagne on ice.
- Brief staff and start them arranging the rooms and setting tables etc.
- Make:
    Watercress Salad
    Carrot and Banana Salad
    Courgette Salad
    Tomato and Onion Salad
    Cucumber and Sour Cream Sauce.
- Finish off:
    Oriental Seafood Salad
    Potato Salad
    Strawberry Romanoff.
- Decorate:
    Salmon Ring Mousse
    Avocado Mouse
    Stuffed Veal.
- Set up the buffet.
- Check the drinks organisation.
- Check that the staff are happy with the set up and make any changes that might be necessary.
- Get coffee ready to make.
- Clear the kitchen ready to do the washing up.
- Check the hire equipment and make a note of any breakages.

## Ground Rules

If the host and hostess are available when you arrive at a venue it is a good idea to run quickly through the arrangements with them so that everyone knows what is expected. You must also establish the ground rules at the start. This is particularly important if you are working in the client's own home.

Establish that the kitchen is yours, fix the time you intend to leave – specially important with an evening party – and deal with the question of leftovers.

The food is the client's since the client has paid for it, but there are exceptions. A cheeseboard, for example, needs a lot of cheese to look attractive but there is probably much more on it than the required number of portions. At other events, the leftovers will not be wanted and you may be able to take them home yourself. If so, remember to take bags and wrappings for them.

It is sensible to stick to the ground rules once established. Go when you said you would. Do as much clearing up in that time as possible; if the guests are still drinking, the clients will have to wash up the glasses. If coffee is not on the menu, resist the kindly impulse to make a quick cup for one guest – the rest will want it!

## Serving the Food

Serving the food at a sit-down meal is fairly straightforward and is dealt with in the section on staff.

A buffet meal, on the other hand, is judged as much by its looks as by its taste. Presentation and the arrangement on the buffet table are very important. Try to make the buffet look as attractive as possible. If the numbers are fairly small you will probably be able to put all, or at least the first two, courses on the table at once, but do make sure that there is plenty of room for access to the buffet and that there is more than one starting point.

If the numbers are large you may only be able to display one course at a time. Flowers, candles and other table decorations can help here. Colour co-ordination and pattern in the table coverings, napkins, flowers and food can also look very effective.

Take advice from your staff on setting things up. They have probably done this many more times than you have and they are experts at their job. They can also help a great deal with regulating the flow of food. If possible, have one or two waitresses serving behind the buffet. They can keep food back for late arrivals at a running buffet and can, if absolutely necessary, stretch things out to feed an unexpectedly expanded number. They can also help to move food on so that the next course can be served.

If there is to be a buffet at a wedding breakfast it is a very good idea to set a separate table, with chairs, for the bridal party as they may be held up with photographs or be wandering round talking to their guests while everyone else wolfs the food.

And it is even more important to organise easy access to the food for a children's party. Manners tend to be forgotten and you cannot expect children to pass on a plate of their favourite goodies. Put the food out on small plates and place them at frequent intervals along the table so that everyone can reach everything.

Another point to remember is to keep the hot food service together. Start by taking round cold items and then, when all the guests have arrived, bring out the hot food and keep it coming for a period of time. You can then ease up, check the quantities remaining and later send out another burst of food.

Clearing away is important for nothing looks worse than piles of discards and half-empty canapé trays. Take the trays back to the kitchen and fill them up. Also make sure that there is somewhere for guests to put their discards, preferably with a mountain of paper napkins beside it. And keep clearing them away.

## Serving the Drinks

Drinks service needs to be planned too. Make sure that you have everything ready and pour out a selection of drinks or wines before the guests arrive. Thus, if a large number arrive together they all get a drink immediately. Allow about twice the number of glasses to guests for a full bar, and about 15–20% extra for wine service. Guests have a habit of finishing their drinks and putting their glasses down. When they want another drink they cannot find their original glasses.

If you are organising a full bar or are serving cocktails, you will need garnishes, so remember to bring cocktail cherries, lemons, oranges, sprigs of mint, stuffed olives, cocktail onions and a supply of cheap but pretty cocktail sticks. Sugar and eggs are also essential if you plan to frost the edges of the glasses – always very effective.

Check off the bar items with whoever is to run it and make a note of replacements as the barman needs them. This helps to keep down fiddling.

# CONTINUOUS ASSESSMENT

It is very easy, if things seem to be going well, to lct your business carry on the way it is, but you should bring your head up out of the sand once in a while and take an overall view of your operation.

Is your estimating still in line with actual costs? Are you on course for increasing or decreasing profitability? Are you changing your menus often enough? Do you need some new promotional ideas or do you have so much business that you need to organise more formal help?

Making sure that you know the answers to these questions every six months or so will help to ensure that you are running a really successful business.

# Appendix

## SPECIALIST SUPPLIERS

*Paper Bags and Boxes, Plastic Bags and Foil Containers*

Cheverton & Laidler Ltd,
Chevler Works,
Princess Risborough,
Bucks.

United Yeast Co Ltd,
Tyseley Industrial Estate,
Selleys Road,
Greet,
Birmingham 4B11 2LD.

Lakeland Plastics Ltd,
Alexandria Buildings,
Station Precinct,
Windermere,
Cumbria LA23 1BQ.

D. J. Parry & Co Ltd,
3–7 Avon Trading Estate,
Avonmore Road,
London W14 8UE.

Bagman of Cantley,
The Old Granary,
Lingwood,
Norwich NR1 4A2.

### Preserving Equipment

George Fowler Lee & Co Ltd,
82 London Street,
Reading,
Berks.

A. W. Gregory & Co Ltd,
Glynde House,
Glynde Street,
London SE4 1R7.

### Sausage Skins

Gynsin & Hanson Ltd,
227–231 Rotherhythe New Road,
London SE16 2BA.

### Smoking Equipment

Brook's Original Home Smokers,
88 Windsor Road,
Southport,
Merseyside.

Frank Odell & Co Ltd,
43–45 Broad Street,
Teddington,
Middlesex.

### Cake Decorating Equipment

Mary Ford Cake Artistry Centre,
28–30 Southbourne Grove,
Southbourne,
Bournemouth BH6 3RA.

# Index